W9-DFG-107

Teaching—
The Imperiled Profession

DANIEL LINDEN DUKE
Lewis and Clark College

Teaching—
The Imperiled Profession

State University of New York Press

ALBANY

Published by
State University of New York Press, Albany

©1984 State University of New York

For information, address State University of New York
Press, State University Plaza, Albany, N.Y., 12246

Library of Congress Cataloging in Publication Data

Duke, Daniel Linden.
    Teaching—the imperiled profession.

    Includes bibliographical references and index.
    1. Teachers—United States—Job stress. 2. Teachers
—United States—Job satisfaction. 3. Teacher morale.
I. Title.
LB2840.2.D85   1984   371.1'0023'73   83-18181
ISBN 0-87395-788-1
ISBN 0-87395-789-X (pbk.)

Contents

To Cheryl Duke

with thanks to Pat Schmuck, Susan Roper, Dennis Sauro, Vern Jones,
Doug Morgan, and Marty Herdener

I long to accomplish a great and noble task, but it is my chief duty to accomplish humble tasks as though they were great and noble. The world is moved along, not only by the mighty shoves of its heroes, but also by the aggregate of the tiny pushes of each honest worker.

—Helen Keller

Part I

Symptoms of Sickness

CHAPTER 1

Domains of Disappointment

Would you teach in a public school today? If you answered with an unqualified "yes," you represent an ever dwindling number of people who still regard teaching as a viable occupation. For many, teaching seems unrewarding and uninspiring. College students no longer flock to education programs. The exodus of burned-out veteran teachers continues, despite uncertain economic conditions.

Who can blame these individuals? Public criticism of education has continued, unabated, for decades. The demands placed on teachers grow even as funds for schools are cut. Teachers are chagrined at the message "Do more with less!" Taxpayers evidence less willingness to support public schooling than at almost any other period in U.S. history. Teachers are attacked symbolically in the press and all too realistically in classrooms and corridors. For all this travail the men and women who are heroic or masochistic enough to teach receive remuneration which often is less than that received by local sanitation workers, teamsters, and automobile mechanics.

A much-needed study is one that probes the reasons why some people continue to teach, despite the poor conditions. This topic is not my present concern, however. Rather, another question prompts this book: Is there reason to believe that teaching as a profession is any less viable today than in the past? Teachers, of course, have always had to cope with criticism, but my reading of educational history fails to find another era when their profession was so imperiled. Until recently, teaching was regarded almost universally as an essential service, a key element in the nation's future. An expanding economy and birthrate ensured teachers a measure of job security. Changes, inside school systems and in the broader socioeconomic context within which schools exist, however, have confronted teachers and prospective teachers with a less-than-enticing career.

In my investigation of the current state of the teaching profession, I draw liberally from the scholarship of Seymour Sarason. In *Work, Aging, and Social Change*, Sarason speculates on the reasons why so

many professionals, despite years of training, are considering changing careers.[1] On the basis of a number of interview studies and a
thorough review of the literature on job satisfaction, he concludes
that changes since the end of the Second World War have increased
the likelihood that what prospective professionals expect of their
careers will fail to correspond with the reality of being a professional.
Professionals are perceived to enjoy substantial autonomy and influence. Their work is presumed to yield considerable self-satisfaction
and positive feelings related to their contributions to the betterment
of society. Being a professional is supposed to entail continuous
intellectual growth and challenge. Professional training and socialization stress the importance of sound judgment, compassion, insight,
creativity, and technical expertise.

The reality of professional work, Sarason argues, deviates markedly
from the expectations of the uninitiated. Professionals increasingly
spend their working lives in large organizations—hospitals, clinics,
law firms with dozens of attorneys. They are subject to procedures,
organization rules, routines, and red tape. Instead of being able to
exercise the professional judgment they spent years in college and
university refining, professionals discover that crass economic considerations often serve as the basis for decisions regarding clients.
Today's professionals, rather than being universally hailed as selfless
servants of the public, are frequently criticized as opportunistic and
egocentric individuals who create as many problems as they resolve.[2]
Instead of growing in their jobs, professionals often complain that
they are "locked in" to dealing with the same set of problems day
in and day out. Tremendous time demands prevent them from
pursuing high quality opportunities for professional development.

The essence, then, of Sarason's thesis is that contemporary professionals are the bearers of a variety of unrealistic expectations, the
possession of which produces disillusionment, job dissatisfaction, and
the yearning to try other fields of endeavor. While Sarason draws
primarily on examples from medicine, law, and university doctoral
programs, it is my contention that his findings also are applicable
to teachers.[3] By investigating what I call "domains of disappointment"—or the *sources* of unrealized expectations—I hope to create
a basis for thinking about reconceptualizing and improving the job
of teaching.

The analyses of teaching that appear in Chapters 3 through 8 focus
on six domains of disappointment—teaching tasks, students, societal
context, higher education, externally based innovation, and professional activities. Each domain encompasses a set of expectations and
a corresponding set of experiential discoveries (reality). An overview

of the domains, along with some illustrative expectations and discoveries, is presented in the accompanying table.

AN APPEAL TO PROFESSIONALS AND POLICYMAKERS

This book has a dual purpose. First, it is intended to provide prospective teachers with an overview of their intended profession, not with a mind to discouraging them from further preparation, but in order to minimize the likelihood that their initial confrontation with school and classroom will be so disillusioning that they abandon teaching altogether. It is my sincere belief that new teachers who are aware of the organizational and societal contexts in which they must work and who understand the nature of their clients are better able to withstand the "induction" period of teaching and eventually participate in the reconceptualization of the profession.

Table 1 Domains of Disappointment for Contemporary Teachers

Domain	Expectations	Reality
Teaching tasks	Autonomy Opportunity to exercise personal judgment Challenging work Goal clarity Security	Rules and procedures (formalization) Routine work Ambiguity regarding goals Insecurity
Students	Motivation to learn Willingness to respond to reason Respect for authority	Apathy Behavior problems
Societal context	Public support and appreciation Adequate resources Professional discretion	Public criticism and impugning of motives Increasing pressure for greater results Diminishing resources Legal and governmental constraints
Higher Education	Training based on technical skills Availability of scholarly assistance Opportunities for continuing professional growth	Training based on general knowledge Research criticizing teachers Trivial in-service programs
Externally based innovation	School improvement is non-political	School improvement is highly political Innovations can leave schools worse off than before
Professional activities	Collegiality Cooperation between teachers Commitment to high ideals	Isolation Competition between teachers Commitment to material self-interests

Of course, new teachers cannot effect major changes alone. Those who participated in or observed the Teacher Corps appreciate this fact. Policymakers and experienced teachers must help, if a viable and challenging profession of teaching is to be built. Therefore, this book also is intended for legislators, educational agency bureaucrats, school administrators, school board members, professors of education, researchers, taxpayers, and teacher union leaders. A tendency exists for some of these individuals to oversimplify the plight of teachers, attributing discontent and questionable performance to lack of talent, low pay, or low status alone. As Table 1 suggests, however, the troubled state of the teaching profession derives from a complex array of factors ranging from those mentioned above to the nature of the work itself and the unfriendly behavior of supposed allies. Efforts by policymakers to assist teachers without recognizing this complexity are probably doomed to failure. Teachers certainly do not need another round of well-intentioned, but misguided reform.

The final two chapters of the book offer a comprehensive set of recommendations for improving the health of the teaching profession. The fact that few of the ideas are new does not diminish the need to present them in a comprehensive way accompanied by a coherent rationale. The inclusion of references to promising contemporary developments in these closing chapters hopefully will offset some of the pessimism present in the first part of the book.

A Note on Sources

The materials upon which this book is based have been gleaned from a variety of sources, including current educational research, articles about teaching in popular magazines and newspapers, interactions with colleagues, and personal observations. I have attempted to sample as much documentation and data as possible, but I recognize that no pretense of thoroughness can be maintained. In deciding what information to give priority status, I again have been influenced by Sarason. He contends that efforts to understand the world of work must rely heavily on the perceptions of workers.[4] While self-reports may not meet all the scientific demands of objectivity, limiting acceptable data to highly controlled observations of what workers do is unlikely to reveal insights concerning *why* particular jobs are satisfying or dissatisfying. Thus, I turn whenever possible to surveys of teacher opinion, interview studies, and personal conversations with teachers. Press coverage of educational issues, while frequently subject to parochialism and sensationalism, is useful to the extent that it reflects the societal context within which teachers live and work. The world of work, it goes without saying, is not the world of the social scientist's laboratory. It is complicated, subjective, and impossible to control.

Having said all this, I obviously cannot claim that *Teaching—The Imperiled Profession* is a neat and narrow research study. The topic is extremely broad, its peripheries blurring occasionally into the formless mass of society-at-large. My purpose is less to prove that a specific set of factors explain all of the discontent expressed by teachers than to identify a set of concerns upon which policymakers might reasonably focus attention in order to forestall any further deterioration in the morale of the teaching profession. I hope that eventually my colleagues in educational research can seek clearer understandings of what it is like to be a teacher today. Sometimes, however, the seriousness of a concern means that action must be taken before the "final word" from the research community is in. I believe the imperiled state of the contemporary teaching profession is just such a concern.

CHAPTER 2

Assessing the Vital Signs

If you are a physician ministering to the needs of ailing professions, where can you look for evidence of illness? One indicator probably is the capacity of a profession to accomplish what it is supposed to accomplish. Thus, if teachers are unable to produce competent students capable of securing employment and advanced education, it can be argued that the health of the teaching profession is questionable.

Other indicators include the ability of a profession to attract qualified newcomers and to retain seasoned veterans. If teaching is failing to recruit bright college graduates or if it cannot induce experienced teachers to stay, the prognosis for the profession once again will be poor.

A final diagnostic strategy is simply to observe members of the profession—look into their eyes, listen to them talk about their work, watch them as they come to and leave the workplace. If they do not look and sound healthy, the probability of sickness is great.

In this chapter I shall take a careful look at some of teaching's vital signs to determine whether it is truly an imperiled profession.

TEACHER PRODUCTIVITY

Teachers are unlike factory workers. They do not produce "things." When they fail to perform their job adequately, it is hard to estimate the cost of ineffectiveness. The goals of public education in the United States are far less precise than the goals of Ford Motor Company or Bethlehem Steel. Teachers, like most other professionals, provide services to clients. As a result of their contact with teachers, these clients—students—are expected to acquire certain skills and knowledge deemed valuable by the society, to learn obedient and responsible behavior, and to obtain gainful employment or advanced education upon graduation. Critics of public education claim that contemporary students are less academically competent, less well-behaved, and less able to function effectively after leaving school than students of previous years. The blame for this perceived situation is attributed to a variety of factors, though the teaching profession receives a substantial portion.

Teachers are accused of devoting less time and attention to the "basics." High school teachers are indicted for offering non-essential electives, lowering their expectations for student achievement, and inflating grades. Observers note the relative scarcity of traditional instructional practices such as drill, recitation, and homework—practices associated in the public mind with student mastery of basic skills.

Evidence of teacher failure to stress the "basics" comes from a variety of sources. An annual ritual for several national news magazines is decrying the decline of student scores of the Scholastic Aptitude Test (SAT), the test many colleges require of applicants. Under such headlines as "Give Us Better Schools" (*U.S. News and World Report*, September 10, 1979), "Help! Teacher Can't Teach" (*Time*, June 16, 1980), and "Drive to Rescue America's Battered High Schools" (*U.S. News & Work Report*, September 8, 1980), figures are presented to indicate the steady decline of SAT scores. From 1962 through 1980 the average score on the verbal section dropped from 478 to 424 and on the mathematics section from 502 to 466.[1] In assessing the impact of steadily declining test scores, two *Los Angeles Times* journalists, in a special report on U.S. schools, expressed what many people perceive to be true:[2]

> The trend seems to indicate that students are losing their ability to handle more complex matters, more sophisticated language, disciplined and articulate written discourse on any given subject, higher mathematical concepts and ideas that demand some critical thought.

In its surveys of student achievement during the seventies the National Assessment of Educational Progress finds further evidence of declining achievement.[3] Between 1972 and 1978, for example, only nine-year-old blacks appreciably improved their scores in mathematics. Achievement dropped for all other groups and significantly so for thirteen-year-old whites and all seventeen-year-olds. Interestingly, in reading achievement the decline was less pronounced. Between 1971 and 1975, achievement declined substantially only for students in urban schools.[4] Reading achievement actually increased for most other categories of students. In science, as in mathematics, though, achievement dropped for almost every category of student between the two testing dates, 1969 and 1973.[5]

Complaining that many of their students are unable to comprehend reading matter of write coherent essays, colleges now require students without requisite skills to take "bonehead English." In some states, college authorities have exerted pressure on public schools to stiffen graduation requirements. Proficiency examinations for all students expecting to earn a high school diploma have been mandated in several states and are being considered in others.

State legislatures and colleges are not alone in their criticisms of teachers. Minority parents condemn teachers for neglecting the special academic needs of their children. Parents of gifted children complain that teachers do not provide sufficient stimulation and challenge.

Student academic achievement is not the only area in which teachers' productivity is perceived to be slipping. Discipline—or students' ability to function in rule-governed settings—also seems to have declined. Reports of truancy, disobedience, and disrespect for authority abound. Teachers are criticized for inconsistent enforcement of school rules, provocative behavior, and failure to establish sufficiently structured environments. Many parents withdraw their children from "undisciplined" public schools and place them in private or parochial schools, which are perceived as providing more order and control.

Many critics also blame inadequate performance by teachers for student lack of preparation for the world of work. The number of dropouts is increasing. One recent report indicated that one student out of every four fails to graduate from U.S. high schools, a statistic which compares unfavorably to the Soviet Union's reported 98 percent graduation rate.[6] Employers complain that they are confronted by large numbers of unskilled job applicants. Large firms have begun to provide their own on-the-job training intended, in large measure, to correct the learning deficiencies of new workers. In addition, they contend that today's workers lack many of the habits that are desired in industry and commerce. These habits range from punctuality to perseverance.

VALID CLAIMS?

The claims briefly reviewed in the preceding section suggest that teachers may not be accomplishing what is expected of them. There can be little disagreement that a profession that fails to live up to popular expectations for performance is in trouble. Before checking out other vital signs for the teaching profession, it may be instructive to consider the validity of these claims of decreasing productivity. In this regard two questions need to be addressed:

1. Are student achievement, behavior, and preparation for the world of work really declining?

2. If students are, in fact, doing less well, can the situation be explained in terms of declining teacher productivity?

Student Performance

It is extremely difficult to prove conclusively that one group of students is performing less capably than a previous group. One reason is that no two groups ever contend with exactly the same sets of circumstances. History refuses to stand still so that high school seniors one year can be easily compared to high school seniors the preceding year.

There may be other reasons in addition to the ever-shifting tide of events that invalidate claims that today's students simply are less skilled and less well-behaved than their predecessors. In order to consider some of these reasons, it may be helpful to rephrase the initial question. If student performance is not actually declining, what factors can account for the "illusion" of decline?

At least three possible factors can be identified: 1) measurement problems, 2) changing expectations, and 3) changes in the student population.

An obvious measurement problem relates to the difficulty of questions on standardized achievement tests. A decline in mean test scores could be due to increasingly difficult test questions. When the College Entrance Examination Board explored this matter with relation to SAT scores, however, it concluded that test questions had not increased in difficulty. If anything, the questions have become easier![7]

Another measurement factor is possible improvements in the reporting of student performance data. Take behavior problems, for example. Students may be misbehaving about as much as they ever have, but if the methods for reporting student behavior problems have improved, then it will appear as if students today are greater discipline problems than those of previous years. While there is general agreement that data collection on discipline problems by school administrators has become more systematic, it is also acknowledged that this fact alone cannot completely account for the steep rise in such problems as truancy, class cutting, assaults, and use of controlled substances on campuses.

A third measurement problem concerns the scope of assessment of student performance. If the tests used to chart the steady decline of student performance cover only a limited range of knowledge and skills, it can be argued that students may be doing as well as or better than before in untested areas. It is true that standardized tests do not encompass a broad range of knowledge and skills. Hence, little is known of how student performance in such subjects as career education, vocational education, problem solving, current events, values, and the arts compares to the past. What does seem to be well-established, though, is the fact that student performance in traditional "core" curriculum areas such as reading, writing, and mathematics has, on the average, decreased.

This decrease could be explained without indicting students' motivation to learn or teachers' ability to teach, however. If the public's expectations for students have steadily increased over the last two decades, then students may actually be out-achieving their predecessors, while still disappointing their parents. There is little doubt that teachers have been compelled to assume many new responsibilities in recent years. These responsibilities—from guaranteeing equal opportunity for girls, the handicapped, and minority students to drug and safety education—constitute a net increase in expectations. However, in areas like English, mathematics, and science, it is hard to determine whether expectations have been subject to inflation. People today do seem to have become so accustomed to growth and progress that it is possible they no longer are satisfied when achievement remains the same from one year to the next. Still, there are strong indications that achievement in core areas actually has declined in an absolute sense, at least for adolescents.

One final reason why the decline may be illusory is a change in the types of students attending public schools in the U.S. The period of perceived decline in student performance coincides with the reaching of adolescence of "baby boom" children, the integration of many schools, and the influx of many non-English-speaking refugees. Secondary school teachers, until very recently, have been faced with unprecedented numbers of students. Teachers at all levels have had to deal with greater varieties of students. Meanwhile, the percentage of "Anglo" students in public schools continues to drop, a fact which can contribute to declining test scores if tests are "culturally biased" or geared to the interests and experiences of white, middle class-students.

I shall return to the issue of changing student population in public schools in Chapter 4. There is no question that this change has had an impact on teaching. Yet, it is clear that the decline in test scores has cut across all groups including white, middle-class students. Is this latter group of students getting less attention from teachers because of the increase of minority students? Is there a cumulative effect related to declining achievement, so that as the concentration of lower achieving students increases the overall rate of teacher effectiveness decreases? Are teachers actually more effective today with some groups of students than they have been in the past?

These and other questions cannot be answered with currently available data. What can be said with some confidence is that large numbers of students served by the public schools are not as skilled in areas such as reading, writing, mathematics, and science as their predecessors are perceived to have been by many educators, college authorities, and employers. Large numbers of students seem to be disobeying school rules with impunity, while school officials find it more difficult than ever before to expel the students. Finally, about one student out of four does not graduate from high school, thus creating a large reservoir of people who are less likely to be in contention for good jobs in the future.

Teacher performance

If many U.S. students are not performing as well as expected, can their plight be attributed to the failure of the teaching profession?

I am obliged to begin with an assumption that underlies all my thinking about education. I do not believe that a process as complex as students' performance is ever the product of a single determining factor. Therefore, any national decline in students' performance must be understood in terms of a multiplicity of influences. It certainly is not unreasonable, though, to suspect that the quality of teaching is a primary contributor. Interestingly, this feeling is shared by many citizens. In a poll designed to identify reactions to declining test scores, it was found that non-educators attributed the decline more to lower quality education than to problems with the tests themselves.[8]

Despite the preceding statement, some educational researchers until recently have tended to downplay the role teachers play in determining student performance.[9] Summarizing much of the literature, John Centra and David Potter conclude,[10]

> that student achievement is affected by a considerable number of variables of which teacher behavior is but one. In fact, so numerous are the factors that influence student growth, that some critics . . . have even argued that teachers have no effect whatsoever on educational outcomes, maintaining instead that students learn primarily because of their own abilities and forces that exist in their personal histories, homes, and communities.
>
> Although this is an extreme position, it does contain an element of truth: teacher effects are likely to be small when compared with the totality of the effects of the other variables affecting student achievement.

In the last decade, educational researchers have begun to study schools and classrooms made up of essentially similar groups of students—similar in terms of their "personal histories, homes, and communities" and their abilities. Often they find that students in certain schools and classrooms out-perform similar students in other schools and classrooms. Having controlled for other factors, the researchers are finding that teachers' characteristics can make a substantial difference.

Richard Murnane, in a review of research on school effectiveness, reports on a variety of teacher-related factors that have been directly linked to students' academic achievement.[11] These factors include teachers' verbal ability, the quality of their preparation, their job experience, and their expectations for students. A team of English researchers studying twelve inner-London secondary schools with comparable student populations lend support to the notion that teachers can make a difference.[12] They found that schools with the worst student behavior problems were characterized by the greatest percentages of inexperienced teachers.

Studies showing that teachers and teaching are related to students' performance appear to confirm the feelings of critics of public schools who are only too willing to blame students' low performance on teachers. There is, of course, a positive dimension to these studies as well. If teachers contribute to low performance, they also must influence students' growth and progress. The ultimate test of how much teachers contribute to students' performance is probably too radical and unethical to be attempted. Such a test would involve comparing the performance of students taught by teachers with that of comparable students not receiving an education from teachers. It is difficult to imagine young people learning better in the absence of teaching than when formal instruction is present.

The analysis to this point reveals a number of inconclusive feelings and a few well-supported beliefs. It is at present impossible to *prove* in any scientific sense that teachers today are less productive than their predecessors. Part of the difficulty lies in the fact that so much about the nature of teaching has been changing over the last twenty years. Some of these changes—from the tasks of teaching to new students and laws—will be explored in upcoming chapters. Still, the fact remains that there is considerable evidence that students are not performing as well as expected in a host of school-related areas. Furthermore, for sound or unsound reasons, many segments of the public perceive that teachers are largely responsible for the situation. The old saying remains true—what is perceived as real is real in its consequences.[13] The consequences of the popular belief that teachers are not as productive as before include a variety of disturbing developments—including decreased fiscal support for schools and increased legislation controlling teachers. These developments can help to create the very situation they presumably are trying to correct.

Low public esteem for teaching also causes experienced teachers to lose confidence in their own abilities. The situation is analogous to a healthy person surrounded by people who constantly tell him he looks ill. Eventually he is likely to begin to believe that he really is ill. Few individuals are so confident of their abilities that they can completely ignore outside judgments. An additional negative consequence is that talented new recruits will shun the teaching profession. These consequences will be discussed in the following sections.

OBSERVING TEACHERS

Statistics concerning teacher productivity can be useful, but a good diagnostician of professional problems need only observe today's teachers to tell that something is woefully wrong.

Look into teachers' eyes. All too often the eyes convey weariness, frustration, and stress—the mask of the quietly desperate. With jobs that are not good enough to justify enthusiasm and not quite bad enough to merit total surrender, thousands of teachers live from day to day, hoping only to get through another seven hours without major incident.

Listen to teachers talk. Rarely are heard comments about improving education—comments so common in the sixties. Today simply being able to "maintain"—to accomplish this year what was done last year—is regarded as a tremendous achievement. Teacher lounges and lunchrooms are filled with talk of early retirement, how students have changed for the worse, and the inexorable flow of new responsibilities and guidelines.

Observe teachers as they go about their work. Actually, observing teachers is not as easy as it once was. Many arrive as late as possible and leave as early as they can. Principals joke about teachers whose cars are out of the parking lot before the afternoon school busses. Teacher absenteeism has reached alarming proportions in many school systems. The December 14, 1981, issue of *Education Week*, in fact, contained a feature-length article entitled "Absent Teachers Cost Schools Billions Yearly." Among other statistics, the article reported that one-quarter of Pennsylvania's school districts experienced an average increase in teacher absenteeism of 44 percent over the nine-year period from 1968–69 to 1977–78. An average of 4.3 percent of a district's teachers (based on a national survey) were absent each day during the 1978–79 school year. Bureau of Labor statistics cited in the article show that the absenteeism rate for all U.S. full-time wage-earners has remained at about 3.5 percent over the last several years. In Philadelphia during 1980–81, teachers missed an average of 16.8 days of school.[14]

Teachers, as well as observers and statisticians, are aware of the ethos of despair in the ranks. Attendance at inservice workshops on stress is steadily growing. In New York in 1979, 51 of 146 disability retirements were for psychiatric or neurologic conditions, a marked increase over previous years.[15] Sabbaticals seem to have replaced by "burnout leaves," as some teachers who do not qualify for early retirement seek respite. In 1979 Tacoma, Washington, became the first district in the nation to provide stress insurance for its teachers.[16]

Efforts to understand the occupational hazards of teaching and to provide assistance are increasing. The American Federation of Teachers has prepared a packet of materials on stress for members and initiated research into the problem. Surveys of teachers indicate that sources of stress range from fear for personal safety to involuntary reassignment.[17] Job stress is reported to contribute to the development of physiological disorders such as hypertension, the breakup of families, and reliance on drugs.

Retention

Given the widespread reports of job-related stress among teachers, it is not surprising that the teaching profession's ability to retain seasoned veterans is being strained. Add to this development the traditional difficulty teaching has had trying to hold young teachers and the prognosis for the profession is gloomy indeed. In 1980 alone it was predicted that 110,000 teachers would drop out of the classroom and seek other employment.[18]

The high turnover rate in teaching has been investigated by numerous researchers.[19] It has also been noted that the individuals who only stay in teaching for a few years before moving on to other occupations often are brighter on the whole than those who stay. Henry Levin indicates that many teachers with high verbal achievement scores on standardized tests leave teaching in the first three years, a particularly distressing fact in light of the positive correlation between teacher verbal ability and student achievement.[20] Only during the depression years from 1930–1940 did teachers with relatively high verbal scores tend to stay in the profession.

In a recent study of North Carolina teachers, Phillip Schlechty and Victor Vance support and extend Levin's findings.[21] They find that by the ninth year of teaching, approximately half of the individuals initially employed to teach remain in education. Further, they observe

. . . a strong negative correlation between measured academic ability and retention in teaching. Year after year, those North Carolina teachers who scored highest on a test of academic ability (the NTE) are the most likely to leave education.[22]

Despite tight economic conditions and high unemployment not unreminiscent of the depression years, many experienced teachers are bailing out of education. The break-up of the stable, core workforce of veteran teachers is one of the most powerful indicators of the profession's imperiled status. Department of Labor statistics show that between 1962 and 1976 the percentage of public school teachers with 20 or more years of experience was cut in half.[23] In a case study of one suburban school district in California, 52 tenured teachers out of a total workforce of less than 450 voluntarily left their jobs between 1978 and 1980.[24] Twenty-five teachers took fulltime leaves of absence, typically to explore new careers or recuperate from burnout. Twenty-one teachers simply resigned, while six more elected early retirement. None of these teachers was in risk of losing his or her job and the district could hardly be characterized as a system in crisis.

The fact is that many of the individuals who have received training as teachers, been licensed, and actually occupied teaching positions are actively considering leaving the profession, despite less than ideal economic conditions. It is not that these teachers are being forced out of teaching by Reductions in Force. As Schlechty and Vance found in North Carolina, brighter veteran teachers are moving on to what they perceive to be more desirable work.[25] The existence of alternative career opportunities cannot totally account for the exodus. A study of female elementary teachers in four school systems across the country found that dissatisfaction with working conditions was also an influence.[26] Forty percent of the teachers sampled in a recent National Education Association survey said they had no intention of remaining in teaching until retirement.[27] One-third indicated that they would not choose a teaching career if they had it to do over again. In another survey, this one conducted by *Learning* magazine, one-quarter of 1,282 teachers reported their intention to leave teaching.[28] Many gave as their reason the increase in job-related stress. When Dworkin analyzed responses from 312 teachers who had left teaching positions in one year in a large city in the Southwest, he discovered that over three-fourths of them cited their reassignment to a school regarded as undesirable as the primary reason for leaving.[29]

When veteran teachers exit, they take with them considerable knowledge of local conditions and students, as well as experience in classroom management and dealing with parents. In addition, they take expertise in subject matter areas that may not be easily replaced. Recent shortages in such areas as mathematics and science are illustrative.

Talented teachers of mathematics and science are in particular demand in private industry. Capitalizing on widespread discontent in education, recruiters from private industry are making active efforts to lure bright teachers away from schools. In the Santa Clara Valley of California, where a large portion of the U.S. computer industry is located, employment agencies expressly designed to recruit teachers are in operation. A recent nationwide study of teacher shortages in mathematics and science conducted by the National Science Teachers Association found that five times more science and mathematics teachers left teaching in 1981 for jobs outside of education than left due to retirement.[30]

To aid veteran teachers looking for alternative careers, an assortment of services are available. Control Data Corporation offers computerized vocational planning services to teachers in branches located in 29 states.[31] Universities and teacher organizations even feel prompted to provide assistance to job-hunting teachers. San Jose State University offers a course entitled "Career Alternatives for Educators." Teacher associations and unions provide career workshops for bewildered members. When these various resources are inadequate, teachers sometimes are so desperate they take matters into their own hands. I interviewed one teacher at Manhattan Vocational and Technical School who promised 500 dollars to anyone who could help him find a job outside of education.

The experienced teachers who opt to leave teaching may have other characteristics in common besides their competence. Anthony Dworkin notes that, more often than not, they come from middle class rather than working class backgrounds.[32] Alfred Bloch, a psychiatrist working with troubled Los Angeles teachers, reports that those who are prone to "battered teacher syndrome" and subsequently to leaves of absence tend to be more passionate, idealistic, and dedicated—characteristics that can be extremely valuable in effective teaching.[33] While the research cited in this section may not be sufficient for sweeping generalizations, it is cause for alarm. The tendencies reported in the preceding pages suggest that the stable core of the teaching profession may increasingly be composed of people for whom few non-educational employment options exist— people of lackluster talents and minimal commitment to working with young people.

Recruitment

When a profession loses many of its brightest and most competent members—both young persons recently graduated from college and skilled veterans with many years of experience, the situation is dangerous. When the same profession is unable to recruit a steady supply of able new persons to fill openings, the situation is critical. Teaching hovers on the brink of such a crisis.

According to recent predictions, from 1984 to 1988 there will be a demand for 861,000 new teachers, but a supply of only 780,000.[34] The number of college graduates majoring in education has steadily declined since 1972, when 317,254 prospective teachers entered the labor market. In 1980, only 172,900 teachers were graduated.[35] The American Association of Colleges of Teacher Education, whose members account for 80 percent of the new teachers trained annually in the U.S., report a 66 percent drop in the average number of bachelor's degrees in education per member institution since 1973.[36] Comparison of results of annual Gallup Polls of the Public's Attitude Toward the Public Schools indicates dwindling interest in teaching as a career. When asked "Would you like to have a child of yours take up teaching in the public schools as a career?" respondents over the past twelve years have replied as follows:[37]

	1969 %	1972 %	1980 %
Yes	75	67	48
No	15	22	40
Don't know	10	11	12

Tellingly, almost the exact same results as the 1980 Gallup Poll were obtained when Phi Delta Kappa asked educators whether they would like a child of theirs to enter teaching as a career![38]

Data from the Educational Testing Service on college-bound seniors in 1982 indicate relatively minor interest in education as a career.[39] Table 2 summarizes the top six preferences:

Table 2. Top Six Intended Areas of Study

	% Males	% Females	% Total
Business and Commerce	17.5	19.8	18.7
Health and Medical	8.5	19.3	14.2
Engineering	22.5	3.8	12.6
Computer Science/Systems Analysis	8.8	6.7	7.7
Social Sciences	7.2	7.3	7.2
Education	2.2	7.4	5.0

Many school districts openly admit difficulty filling teaching positions. New York City and Los Angeles have thousands of unfilled positions.[40] Large city districts are not alone in having difficulty finding teachers. Small schools have big problems locating sufficient teachers to cope with turnover rates that average twice as much as bigger schools.[41] Doris Helge, Director of the National Rural Project, reports that 94 percent of the states participating in her program experienced "severe" difficulties recruiting and retaining rural teachers.[42] Active recruiting campaigns conducted by urban districts on a nationwide basis also fail to turn up sufficient applicants. In 1979 the National Center for Education Statistics reported that 23 percent of the districts with job openings were unable to fill one or more positions with permanent teachers.[43]

The shortage of new recruits is particularly alarming in the areas of mathematics and science. Of the more than 400,000 students in California's public four-year institutions in the spring of 1982, only 97 were preparing to be secondary mathematics teachers and only 174 were preparing to be secondary science teachers.[44] Among the statistics summarized in an *Education Week* special feature are the following:

- Shortages of qualified mathematics teachers were reported in 43 states in 1981; similar shortages exist for science teachers.
- Among newly appointed science and mathematics teachers last year, 50.2 percent were judged "unqualified" by their principals.[45]

The fear, then, is not only that the supply of teachers will be inadequate, particularly in certain subject matter areas, but that those who do opt for teaching will not be very talented. W. Timothy Weaver has studied the standardized test scores for college-bound high school seniors planning to major in education, college seniors actually majoring in education, and education majors interested in graduate school.[46] In all cases, the average scores for persons interested in teaching careers were well below the average for all students tested. When Weaver analyzed data from the National Longitudinal Study, he discovered that education majors who obtained teaching jobs scored lower on tests of reading and vocabulary competence than education majors who did not find teaching jobs. Weaver concluded that the brightest education majors were going into non-education occupations.

Phillip Schlechty and Victor Vance provide corroborating data.[47] Their analysis of SAT scores for a nationa cohort of 1,177 prospective teachers found that a disproportionately large share of low scores and a disproportionately small share of high scores were represented among those actually electing to teach. Somewhat pessimistically, the researchers determined,[48]

As a practical matter, it is unrealistic to expect that teaching could ever be made sufficiently attractive to those who score in the upper 25% on measures of academic ability to draw into its ranks a proportionate number of these individuals.

Traditionally the teaching profession could rely on bright women to provide a corps of competent teachers, but opportunities for women outside of teaching have expanded dramatically in the past two decades. They no longer constitute a "captive labor market" with few options other than teaching. From 1966 to 1979, interest in teaching careers for freshman women declined from 16 percent to 7 percent (elementary) and from 18 percent to 3 percent (secondary).[49] At the same time, interest in business careers climbed from 3 percent to 17 percent and in professions like law from 6 percent to 26 percent. In their North Carolina study, Schlechty and Vance discovered that most of the decline in academic ability on the part of beginning teachers was accounted for by the decline in academic ability of white females.[50] Clearly, brighter white women are opting for non-teaching careers.

TEACHERS IN TROUBLE

In 1981, the average American public-school teacher was older, had spent more time in college, was relatively less well paid, and was far less likely to choose teaching as a career if given a second chance than was the case in 1976.

So read a summary in *Education Week* (March 10, 1982) of the National Education Association's nationwide survey, entitled *The Status of the American Public School Teacher, 1980–81*. Between 1976 and 1981, the average age for teachers increased from 36 to 39. While 48.7 percent of the 1976 cohort said they would stay in teaching until retirement, only 34.7 percent of the 1981 sample were similarly inclined. Teachers earned considerably more money, on the average, than they had five years before, but not enough to keep pace with inflation.

As the organized teaching profession thus enters its second century, the signs of trouble abound. Large segments of the public believe that students today are less competent and disciplined than their predecessors. These individuals are only too willing to attribute the situation to low quality teaching. Teachers, both talented newcomers and seasoned veterans, are leaving the profession. Those who remain in classrooms often exude an air of weariness, bewilderment, and chagrin. Fewer college students display an interest in becoming teachers, and those who do typically are not to be numbered among the brightest of their class.

Teaching, of course, certainly is no stranger to professional problems. For at least a century teachers have confronted insufficient remuneration and public criticism. But low salaries could always be balanced against the satisfactions of the work itself. And public criticism was offset by praise and support from a variety of sources. Today teachers live in a different world. The pleasures of pedagogy pale next to a growing list of perplexities. The job of teaching is held hostage by conflicting sets of expectations. Students have changed—they seem less motivated to study and less mindful of rules. Teachers are more vulnerable to the vicissitudes of political and community interests. When teachers look for help, they find that the agencies and individuals that are supposed to provide assistance are either ineffectual or actually hostile. As a result, the costs—both psychic and concrete—of being a teacher in public education today have steadily climbed, while the benefits become less and less apparent.

The thesis of this book, then, is that public school teaching has never before been so close to being an impossible profession. Traditionally beset by its share of problems, teaching nonetheless commanded enough popular acceptance and generated enough *esprit de corps* to remain a viable undertaking. I maintain that fairly recent changes—most occurring within the last two decades—have altered this situation. These often complex and poorly understood developments, combined with such longstanding problems as low pay, low status, and public criticism, presently constitute a set of powerful disincentives for employed and prospective teachers.

The image I get of teaching is that of a profession locked in a downward spiral. No longer can cause and effect be easily distinguished. Declining teacher effectiveness can be as much a result of public criticism as a target for it. Changes in students may contribute to teacher troubles as well as reflect lowered professional competence. As it becomes more difficult to separate the causes and effects of teachers' troubles, the downward spiral accelerates and the prognosis for the profession grows increasingly dismal. It is my sincere hope that, by alerting policymakers and educators to some of the important sources of teaching troubles before they become completely obscured by their consequences, the downward spiral process can be arrested.

Part II

Changing Conditions of Work

CHAPTER 3

Ambiguity and Insecurity: The Trying Task of Teaching

The total workweek for all teachers averages 46.1 hours. Teachers have on the average a required school week of 36.3 hours, with an average required school day of 7.26 hours. In addition, all teachers devote a mean of 8.5 hours per week to noncompensated, school-related activities and a mean of 9.6 hours to compensated activities.

The average length of teachers' lunch periods has decreased since 1966, from 38 to 35 minutes.[1]

Teaching is not and has never been an easy job. Teachers always have had to carry their work and worries home with them at night. Sufficient time to minister to the needs of and extract the potential from each student has never been available. Teaching is a profession where the responsibility is great, the potential for failure significant, the remuneration small, and the reinforcement sporadic. In return for caretaking the hopes and aspirations of the nation's young people, teachers have received wages that even missionaries might malign.

Despite the obvious tribulations of the job, teaching traditionally has offered its share of rewards. Rather than merely a job, teaching was regarded as a "calling." Teachers often enjoyed relatively high status, due in large part to the fact they were among the few members of the community with a college education. Working with young minds left one with a sense of contributing to the future of society. Teachers typically did not arise in the morning questioning the worth of their endeavors. An ethos of professionalism surrounded teaching—parents and students accorded teachers respect, the classroom was a teacher's castle, and general agreement about what teachers were expected to accomplish existed.

Larry Cuban recently looked back at high school instruction since 1900 and concluded that it was remarkably persistent and invulnerable to change.[2] Perhaps the net result of scanning more than four score years is to discover constancy, but at a given point in time—particularly any point over the last 20 years—teaching would appear to many participants to have been in a state of flux. Contrary to Cuban, the thesis of this chapter is that the nature of teachers' work has changed sufficiently over the last few decades to alter the traditional configuration of costs and benefits. Gone is the protected environment of the classroom. No longer can teachers be assured of respect from most students or parents. Even the expectations of what teachers are to accomplish and how they are to go about it have become confused. Teachers today must grapple with an increasingly complex array of guidelines and mandates. In return for their efforts, teachers continue to be paid relatively poorly. What is more, they cannot even count on job security. Declining enrollments and public demands for frugality cause even veterans to be alarmed.

In this chapter I shall focus on two disturbing developments in teachers' work: growing ambiguity over what the job of teaching is supposed to entail and increasing sources of insecurity for employed teachers. Perhaps more than any other aspects of the job, ambiguity and insecurity epitomize the discrepancy between expectations and reality that has come to characterize teaching.

AMBIGUITY: FEW COMMON PURPOSES AND TOO MANY PANACEAS

No matter where one looks today, an observer is likely to encounter an opinion about what goals teachers should be pursuing and how to improve teaching effectiveness. The problem for the profession is that the goals and prescriptions often vary considerably. In a rational world, policymakers would reach agreement about the purposes to be served by teachers before selecting particular strategies for improving teaching. The world of the educator is less rational than political, however. As a result, decisions are made concerning panaceas despite the lack of consensus over goals. In a political world, more of a premium is placed on action—even misguided action—than logic and deliberation.

To study the various efforts aimed at helping teachers do a better job is to confront a wide range of motives and working assumptions. To facilitate discussion I have condensed these panaceas into four principle sets of suggestions: job reduction, job simplification, job expansion, and job enrichment. The difficulty with multiple and sometimes conflicting solutions concerns choice. Too many options and the lack of clear-cut favorites breed uncertainty, which in turn can induce stress and undermine the confidence of the very individuals who are targeted for assistance in the first place.[3]

Job Reduction

The first set of suggestions for helping teachers calls for a quantitative change in the tasks of teaching. Job reduction describes the process by which the number of teaching responsibilities or tasks is decreased. Thus, in the midst of the era of social reforms in the late sixties, Larry Cuban challenged the emerging notion that teachers must be social workers and political activists as well as instructors.[4] The assumption underlying this approach is that teachers are more likely to be effective if they have fewer duties.

Job reduction has resulted primarily from two movements: collective bargaining and the use of paraprofessionals in classrooms.

Since 1960 teachers have won the right to negotiate their contracts in most of the country, with the notable exception of the South. In the majority of states where collective bargaining is permitted, teachers are able to negotiate working conditions as well as salaries and benefits. Through this mechanism teachers have pressed for several types of job reduction.

First, they have tried to limit the number of non-instructional duties that can be required without remuneration. Where agreements have been reached, teachers no longer can be required, as a condition of employment, to volunteer for extracurricular activities. Remuneration schedules for duties such as coaching and club sponsorship are specified in many contracts.

Second, teachers have fought to eliminate certain non-instructional duties which they traditionally regarded as onerous and unprofessional. Primary among these duties are those associated with discipline. Contracts now control the amount of non-classroom supervision which can be required of teachers. In a few states teachers also have won the right to suspend obstreperous students from class for several days. Thus, they do not have to function as school disciplinarians. The general thrust of negotiated job reduction has been to confine teacher duties to instruction, planning, evaluation, and classroom management.

Job reduction efforts have been facilitated in many schools by the employment of paraprofessionals. These individuals need not possess a college education in most cases. They often live in the communities from which students come. Paraprofessionals perform functions ranging from taking roll to grading assignments to running off worksheets on the ditto machine. On occasion they also cover classes and handle behavior problems, though state laws often prohibit such delegation of responsibility to non-certificated staff.

The employment of paraprofessionals typically is linked directly to the existence of external funds, such as those derived from federal

Chapter I aid for schools with large numbers of disadvantaged students. When funds disappear so do paraprofessionals. Seasoned teachers learn not to rely too heavily on the presence of additional staff to reduce their workload. Economic retrenchment in the early eighties also is causing the renegotiation of many contracts, with the result that some previously reduced responsibilities are being resumed.

Job Simplification

Job simplification represents a qualitative change in what teachers do. This category subsumes any change that renders teaching tasks easier, less responsible, or less ambitious. The assumption underlying many moves to simplify the job of teaching is that teachers are insufficiently skilled or motivated to undertake challenging tasks.

Job simplification has taken three primary forms: standardization of the curriculum, formalization of rules and procedures, and technological innovation.

Jerome Bruner gained the dubious honor of authoring the notion of the "teacher-proof" curriculum. An outgrowth of the post-Sputnik curriculum reform movement of the early sixties, the teacher-proof curriculum supposedly constituted an antidote to the poor quality instruction which allegedly had allowed the Soviet Union to outstrip the United States in the space race. Arguing that teachers too often strayed from textbooks and failed to challenge young minds, Bruner and his cohorts designed problem-oriented curricula that progressed systematically from one specific objective to the next. Teachers were told to function as guides, helping students move steadily through the elaborately designed texts and workbooks in mathematics, biology, chemistry, physics, and other subjects.

The spirit of the curriculum reform movement has carried on into the seventies and early eighties in the form of behavioral objectives, criterion-referenced testing, programmed texts, mastery learning, competency based education, and proficiency tests. All of these developments can be viewed as efforts to standardize what is taught in American schools. All provide a relatively simple basis for determining whether teachers have deviated from the prescribed curriculum. A third feature shared by these schemes is the minimal involvement of teachers in planning and conceptualizing the goals of instruction.

A second move intended to simplify the job of teaching has entailed the development of formal rules and procedures to guide instructional practice. Concerned over inconsistency among teachers, school administrators and often teachers themselves have called for guidelines covering everything from the evaluation and reporting of student performance to the resolution of student behavior problems. While rhetoric about treating every student as a unique individual continues to be heard, many schools in reality seem to expend more effort ensuring that all students receive the same treatment. Treating all clients similarly—a practice referred to as universalism by organization theorists—lies at the heart of bureaucratic practice. It is one of the features distinguishing the behavior of bureaucrats from that of professionals.

Impetus for formalizing educational practice often has come from outside the schools. With the proliferation of school-related court decisions and educational legislation have come a variety of guidelines and regulations. They cover everything from fair treatment for handicapped and female students to the due process rights of students. While the net effect of all the guidelines and regulations has been anything but simplification, taken separately they constitute attempts to simplify the job of teaching by restricting the discretionary authority of teachers.

The third example of job simplification is embodied in the growing use of high technology in classrooms. From "Sesame Street" to pocket calculators, from filmstrips to microcomputers, technological innovations have altered the traditional patterns of student reliance on teachers. Today, some students can even learn almost entirely in the absence of a teacher. Others need teachers only to give initial instructions on how to operate machines and to see that the machines are in good working condition.

While many teachers have welcomed these sources of job simplification, others complain about the decreasing challenge of the job and their growing sense of alienation. They feel more like "glorified babysitters" and "custodians" than professionals whose judgments and unique skills are critical to student progress. In critiquing recent trends, UCLA Dean John Goodlad observes that student apathy can only be counteracted by the encouragement of teacher "inventiveness," not by emphasizing "homogenized textbooks and workbooks" and a "narrow range of teaching techniques."[5] Noted researcher N.L. Gage, himself a onetime supporter of job simplification, has similarly concluded:

> These innovations reduce the amount of disorder in what the teacher does. But they go too far in a good direction. Because they spell out both the content and procedure of the teachers' work in great detail, they impose too much inflexibility on the teacher. . . . Teachers cannot accept complete regimentation through programming of their behavior. What they teach

requires more room for spontaneity, creativity, and artistry than such programming allows.[6]

Job Expansion

For teachers concerned that teaching is becoming too simple, job expansion offers cold comfort. Job expansion represents a quantitative change in the job of teaching—an increase in the number of duties or responsibilities. There are several assumptions that can be used to support job expansion. One is economic: money is tight and cuts have to be made, but they should be made everywhere except the classroom. As a result of such reasoning, services once performed by support staff are shifted to teachers when the former individuals lose their jobs. A second assumption can be that schools must become the locus of many functions traditionally performed elsewhere. Teachers, by virtue of their close proximity to students, often are the obvious candidates for undertaking these new functions.

In the last decade declining enrollments, inflation, court-ordered efforts to redistribute educational resources and tax-cutting initiatives have caused many school systems to retrench. After years of expanding facilities, hiring more personnel to fill more specialized positions, and increasing programs, school officials have had to rethink how resources are to be allocated. Generally, the principle that "teachers are the last to go" has guided retrenchment decision making.[7] Thus teachers have watched as custodians, attendance clerks, secretaries, curriculum coordinators, campus supervisors, paraprofessionals, librarians, nurses, school psychologists, department heads, security guards, social workers, and community liaisons lost their jobs. Guidance counselors have not even escaped the ax. For example, some California districts reduced or eliminated entirely guidance services following Proposition 13, an amendment to the state constitution which limited the capacity of Boards of Education to generate revenues from property taxes.

As a result of personnel cuts, teachers frequently find themselves being asked to assume additional responsibilities. These responsibilities range from patrolling corridors to phoning parents to check on absent students, from copying worksheets to cleaning rooms. Pat Robinson, a widely respected kindergarten teacher with twenty years of experience in Palo Alto schools, described the impact of Proposition 13 cuts in the following way:

> Well, if I want my floor done, if I want the paint mopped off it that gets spilled, I have to do it myself. Imagine sharing a

room with 28 children everyday. That's an incredible idea. It's crazy, and to not have custodial help everyday. . . .
We've had to take our time to do the custodial work and we've had to train children to do it. . . .[8]

Cuts in non-teaching personnel cannot always absorb all the revenue loss experienced by some school systems. Teachers then must be fired. Decisions typically are made to terminate non-essential programs—for example, courses which are not required by the state for students receiving diplomas. At one high school in San Jose, California, retrenchment led to the elimination of fourteen teachers and, with them, forty-four class sections.[9] Classes in art, music, English as a Second Language, remedial reading, industrial arts, and science were cancelled. In some cases, such as ESL and reading, the teachers who remained were compelled to assume responsibilities previously undertaken by specialists. It is not uncommon to encounter high school teachers who are asked to teach four or five different preparations. Trying to plan simultaneously for subjects as varied as business mathematics and art pushes to the limits the energies of even the best teachers. Elementary teachers also have been faced with job expansion as a result of cuts in teacher specialists in areas such as physical education and the arts.

Retrenchment-related job expansion can be viewed as a form of penalizing survivors. Teachers who are "fortunate" enough to keep their jobs following budget cuts are expected to assume many duties previously performed by departed colleagues.

A second form of job expansion results from a more positive impetus—the belief that teachers are well-suited to undertake certain critical tasks. One such task is student advisement. Alternative schools and school improvement programs such as Individually Guided Education call on teachers to take charge of advising groups of students each year. Advisement can cover everything from transient problems to the choice of a college or career. Teachers are felt to be more familiar with students and their academic work than guidance counselors, whose caseloads of four and five hundred students plus testing and recordkeeping duties often prevent them from staying "in touch" with individual students.

Teachers also are finding themselves asked to undertake more administrative duties. Coordinating the efforts of other adults—such as volunteers or paraprofessionals—is one such administrative task. Another involves directing special programs. With the increase in categorical aid from state and federal government, schools in the sixties and seventies were compelled to set up management systems to oversee, coordinate, and evaluate a host of externally-funded programs. Programs ranged from migrant education to mainstreaming handicapped students, from Title I reading programs to bilingual education. Teachers were invited to supervise these programs, which tended to run for a few years before funds ran out or the program was fully institutionalized. More recently, as school systems cope with retrenchment, administrators have been replaced in many cases by less expensive "teachers on special assignment." These individuals assume many of the responsibilities once reserved for vice principals, including scheduling, teacher evaluation, and discipline.

The growth of alternative schools, including specialized schools-within-schools, has created yet a third new administrative role for some teachers. Often alternative schools will function with a few part-time or full-time teachers and a teacher-coordinator to handle managerial tasks and secure resources.

There are other impetuses to job expansion besides retrenchment and the desire to use teacher skills more extensively. For example, the rise of powerful teacher associations and unions has fostered a plethora of new duties for teachers, many of them involving the assumption of leadership. The job of teaching also has been affected by increased emphasis on staff development. As the average age for teachers climbs, the need for periodic retraining becomes more critical. Teachers are called on to become students again and in some cases, teachers-of-teachers. Teachers are playing a big role in local and regional teacher centers providing educators with workshops and courses covering such topics as classroom management, new court mandates, and special education.

Job expansion for teachers, at least in theory, need not be a particularly negative development. Having a wider range of duties can be challenging and stimulate continued personal and professional growth. All too often, though, job expansion leads to the over-taxing of already strained teacher energies. Part of the perversity of pedagogy seems to be that teachers who are successful with especially difficult assignments are "rewarded" with additional difficult assignments. The classic example of this phenomenon involves the teacher who one year is assigned several students known to cause discipline problems. If the teacher handles these students effectively, the likelihood is great that he or she will continue to be assigned problem students, probably in increasing numbers.

Another example of "punishing" successful teachers concerns leadership duties. It is common for most of the challenging non-instructional assignments in a school to be performed by a handful of energetic and bright individuals. As the number of these talented teachers decreases—due to factors previously discussed—those few who remain in classrooms will be called on the assume a growing proportion of responsible new assignments. Such a development may only serve to accelerate the departure of talented, but overworked teachers.

Job Enrichment

A qualitative change in teaching, job enrichment encompasses efforts to make specific tasks more challenging, complex or responsible. It is just the opposite of job simplification. One possible assumption underlying many instances of job enrichment is that teachers are more capable than they have been given credit for. Upgrading the quality of the tasks of teaching thus may be regarded as a way to keep greater numbers of talented teachers committed to classroom instruction.

Several of the previous examples of job expansion entailed job enrichment, notably those in which teachers were asked to assume administrative duties. Teacher leadership also has been called for in other areas, including school policy making and curriculum development. Teachers traditionally have been granted only limited opportunities to provide input into these processes. Recently, however, concerted efforts have been made in many schools to change the nature of this involvement from advisory to fully participatory. Several research studies in recent years have found a positive correlation between teacher decision-making and student achievement.[10]

Many federal and state programs now require teachers to sit on policy boards and steering committees. In California and Florida attempts to develop systematic school improvement programs center on individual schools. Approximately half of each school site council is expected to consist of teachers.

Job enrichment also has affected what goes on within the classroom. Instruction has become a more complex and demanding process as a result of efforts to individualize instruction, implement diagnostic-prescriptive teaching, mainstream handicapped students, and integrate students from various racial and ethnic backgrounds. Teachers are called on to eliminate instances of sex and racial bias from curriculum materials and avoid communicating lower expectations to students from disadvantaged backgrounds.

At first, job enrichment seems as if it should be hailed by teachers as long overdue recognition of their competence and professionalism. It is somewhat surprising, in fact, to discover that many teachers take a skeptical view of some of these efforts. In certain cases suspicion may be well-founded, however. For instance, attempts to involve teachers in collegial evaluation may be less of an acknowledgement of teacher responsibleness than an indirect way to generate greater supervisory control. Differentiated staffing plans, while they do provide select teachers with challenging, quasi-administrative opportunities, threaten to force "regular classroom teachers to assume the role of technicians."[11]

Insincere attempts to increase teacher authority may be characterized as "co-opting the culprit." In other words, the strategy of school officials is to encourage teachers to play a more significant role in correcting problems which they are perceived to have caused or contributed to in the first place. So if teachers are perceived to be unsuccessful in controlling student misconduct, they may find themselves being invited to plan an inservice workshop on classroom management or develop a school discipline code.

A second somewhat negative impetus to job enrichment might be dubbed the "Who wants to be captain of the Titanic?" approach. Many teachers sense that administrators are only willing to share real decision making authority when the situation has gotten so desperate that they have no choice. Perhaps it is no coincidence that recent efforts to encourage greater teacher involvement in decision making have occurred concurrently with the intensification of public criticism of schools and the beginning of serious fiscal retrenchment in education.

Many teachers are savvy enough to recognize such job enrichment tactics as thinly veiled attempts by administrators to protect themselves. In one study of five California secondary schools, my colleagues and I found that more than half the teachers reported being uninvolved in school decision making, despite various formal opportunities to do so.[12] They saw great benefits to shared decision making, but did not believe that administrators were sincere in wanting to relinquish a significant measure of authority.

Classroom Management: Case Study in Confusion

The coexistence of four relatively distinct efforts to revise the job of teaching confronts teachers with a confusing array of mixed messages, difficult-to-assess alternatives, and contradictory expectations. Nowhere is the confusion greater than the area of classroom management.

Elsewhere I have defined classroom management as the provisions and procedures necessary to establish and maintain an environment in which teaching and learning can occur.[13] One critical dimension of classroom management is the resolution of student behavior problems. These problems—ranging from talking out-of-turn to assault—can seriously impede the accomplishment of instructional objectives and jeopardize the safety of students and teacher alike. The exact role teachers are supposed to play in creating and maintaining a safe and productive environment has become increasingly vague, however.

Individuals who advocate job reduction, for example, contend that teachers are neither paid nor trained to do police work. Among those pressing for a reduction in teacher disciplinary responsibilities are negotiators for teacher organizations. In many states, teachers have won the right to suspend disruptive students from class without administrative approval. They also have obtained assurances that their intervention is not expected when personal safety is in danger. As a result, teachers may not be called on to break up fights, accost menacing strangers on campus, or patrol isolated parts of school grounds.

To offset these efforts to limit teacher involvement in handling student misconduct, more resource people have been employed in many schools.[14] Security guards and campus supervisors control out-of-class behavior problems. School social workers and community liaisons maintain direct contact with the families of troubled students. Guidance counselors, deans of students, assistant principals, and school psychologists often specialize in disciplinary problems. Students themselves have even been involved in disciplinary activities. Student courts, peer counseling groups, and student monitors can be found in many schools.

Ironically, as the number of resource people concerned with student behavior problems has grown, it has become more difficult to locate any single school employee willing to assume ultimate responsibility for helping a particular student. Specialization and increased division of labor, in other words, have not necessarily brought more effective school discipline.

A second approach to improve classroom management entails job simplification. Teachers are counseled to streamline and systematize their disciplinary duties in order to minimize the amount of time devoted to behavior problems. Training programs such as Assertive Discipline and Logical Consequences urge teachers to establish classroom rules and enforce them consistently.[15] Students are regularly reminded of rules and the consequences for disobeying them. If a student disobeys a rule, he or she suffers the specified consequences. Such an approach transforms handling behavior problems from a relatively complex process entailing phone calls home, meetings with counselors, and teacher-student conferences to a simple matter of determining when a rule is broken and meting out a punishment.

Contrary to the spirit underlying efforts to reduce and simplify classroom management is the pressure to expand and enrich teacher involvement in handling student behavior problems. Expansion advocates call on teachers to assume more responsibilities related to discipline, including counseling troubled students, scheduling case conferences, notifying parents, and developing schoolwide rules. Those who push for job enrichment suggest that teachers need to alter the nature of their classroom leadership. Teachers are told to model effective conflict resolution behavior and incorporate discussions of values and appropriate conduct into their regular lessons. In addition, they are advised to regard problems as opportunities. In other words, if a student behaves in a disruptive manner, he or she actually may be communicating to the teacher an upset about some legitimate concern. A perceptive teacher who realizes this fact may be able to help the student more through listening than imposing a punishment.

There are compelling reasons why teachers should and should not support each of the preceding efforts to redefine the tasks of classroom management. In an era when teachers are expected to accomplish more with less, any suggestion that promises to reduce or simplify their responsibilities is alluring. On the other hand, such suggestions tend to routinize teaching and support the contentions of critics that today's teachers are not sufficiently competent to handle student misconduct. Expansion and enrichment recommendations convey faith in the skills of teachers to handle challenging situations more creatively, but they require more time and energy. They also increase the likelihood of failure.

Teachers thus are confronted with a variety of alternatives for managing student behavior problems. Similarly, in areas such as curriculum design, teaching methods, evaluation of student achievement, and the use of high technology, teachers today are faced with more options than ever before. Each option comes with its sales pitch, list of endorsements, and supporting data. Each option promises to improve the job of teaching. In addition, as economic conditions tighten, the competition between developers, change agents, and consultants intensifies. Exaggerated claims are made for particular strategies, and unrealistic expectations are fostered.

The problem with the existence of so many alternatives is how to make the right choice. Decades ago there were few alternatives and fewer factors to be considered when selecting one. Now teachers must weigh an assortment of factors before making a choice. These factors may range from contract violations to legal liability issues, from student rights to state mandates. Choice-making becomes a highly stressful and time-consuming process. Albert Shanker, President of the United Federation of Teachers, warns that teachers are reaching the limits of how much innovation they can manage.[16] The impact of well-intentioned changed efforts on the environments in which teachers work is the subject of a more detailed analysis in Chapter 7. For now, let it suffice to say that some teachers react to the proliferation of new ideas by not choosing any of them. They have witnessed the coming and going of so many panaceas that they no longer believe anything makes a difference. In other cases, teachers select an approach, but are unable to fully commit to it because of their knowledge of other possibilities.

Should teachers strive to be civil servants slavishly following procedures and trying to treat all clients the same? Should they counter public criticism with an aggressive professionalism that demands greater responsibilities rather than seeking the safety of diminished duties? The proliferation of pedagogical panaceas has served to undermine traditional conceptualizations of the job of teaching without replacing them with any clear-cut, universally accepted notion of what teachers should be doing instead. Teachers, like anyone else, find it extremely difficult to combat criticism when they themselves are uncertain about what their job should entail. Uncertainty clearly is not what most individuals expect to find when they enter teaching.

LIVING WITH INSECURITY

If the world of economics functioned according to theory, one might anticipate that teachers, in exchange for tolerating a high degree of ambiguity over the nature of their work and considerable outside criticism, could expect satisfactory compensation and other forms of job security. Obviously, such is not the case. In this section, I survey three sources of insecurity to which contemporary teachers are heir: job insecurity, assignment insecurity, and financial insecurity.

Job Insecurity

Teaching jobs often are regarded by the public as sinecures, relatively well-paid, secure positions requiring little work. Anyone who has actually spent time in a classroom working with students, particularly poorly motivated or low achieving students, realizes how spurious is the claim that teaching is easy. As for the belief that teachers receive a good salary, it has been acknowledged by economists for years that teachers were poorly paid. Recent indications are that they may even be losing ground.

While hardly a sinecure, teaching traditionally did promise a measure of job security. With the exception of a handful of notorious districts that routinely fired probationary teachers rather than granting them tenure and paying them more money, school systems tended to offer most teachers the prospect of steady employment until retirement. This situation has changed dramatically in recent years.

In many districts with collective bargaining, teachers are working without new contracts because agreement cannot be reached about how best to moderate the impact of diminishing resources. Declining enrollments, inflation, and taxpayer insistence on austerity have led to widespread Reductions in Force (RIF's in the jargon of the times). For example, following the passage of Proposition 2½ in Massachusetts in 1980, Quincy and Malden each released 300 of their 1,000 teachers.[17] Statewide, 8,500 out of 70,000 teachers were RIFed between 1980 and 1982. An annual ritual for experienced teachers in many localities across the U.S. is waiting for the spring letter from the superintendent notifying them that their positions may be eliminated. These letters typically are sent to more teachers than actually will be RIFed because school officials must allow themselves some leeway in estimating enrollments for the following autumn. Contracts with teachers generally do not permit fall job termination unless notification has been received the preceding spring.

In districts where the economic or enrollment situation is difficult to predict, hundreds of teachers may receive notifications of possible termination. The year following the passage of Proposition 13 in California, San Francisco and San Jose sent spring letters to virtually all teachers. The impact on a thirty-year veteran teacher of receiving a notification of possible termination is shock and anger. For other teachers—ones more likely to be let go—the period following receipt of spring notices is marked by anxiety and low morale. It is difficult to concentrate on classroom instruction or plan ahead for fall courses. Many teachers begin searching for other jobs.

I have spoken with experienced teachers who each year say goodbye to colleagues with fewer years in the school system. They speak of the difficulty of seeing talented teachers and close friends depart. They also describe their uneasiness as each year they see their own names move nearer the top of the list of candidates for termination. The strain is immense, even for those whose jobs, realistically, seem safe. With declining enrollments predicted for years to come in many districts, the likelihood of continued strain for survivors is great.

Assignment Insecurity

The teachers whose seniority permits them to hang onto positions not only must adjust to uncertainty, but they must face the prospect of receiving assignments they would not choose under normal conditions. Take Marilyn Pesetzky, for example. A teacher in bucolic Putnam Valley, New York, she has worked for the same district thirteen years. While she has taught grades six through nine, she prefers the ninth grade and believes she is most effective with that age group. Declining enrollments caused her to be reassigned to the sixth grade three years ago. Being a conscientious professional, Pesetzky tried to refamiliarize herself with the sixth grade curriculum and do the best job she could. Each year, however, she asks for a ninth grade position. Each year she hears the same reply. "But you're doing such a good job where you are."

Pesetzky is caught in a double bind. If she stops trying to be effective, she risks losing her own self-esteem as well as receiving a poor performance rating. If she continues her competent teaching of sixth graders, she will undermine any claim she has to a ninth grade position. That a professional with thirteen years of effective service should be subject to pawn-like moves by school officials hardly seems reasonable. She cannot help but ask the question so frequently heard among contemporary teachers—"Is it worth it?"

In order to keep their jobs, teachers like Marilyn Pesetzky are being compelled to make a variety of enervating readjustments. Sometimes they are forced to teach an assortment of unrelated subjects in order to keep their jobs. Sometimes they even have to teach subjects for which they have not been trained. In California it is not unusual to find situations in which a teacher with one year's additional seniority will "bump" another teacher, despite the fact they have completely different subject matter specialities. In one of the few systematic studies of teacher dissatisfaction related to misassignment, researchers in British Columbia found that over 12 out of every 100 teachers were officially misassigned and nearly 43 percent were displeased with their assignment.[18] This study was done in 1969, prior to deteriorating economic conditions that doubtless have fostered even greater misassignment.

While being compelled to teach multiple or unfamiliar subjects creates problems for survivors, these pale next to the problems posed by involuntary transfers. In few cases are such transfers made to "preferred" schools. Openings tend to exist at troublespots, schools with lots of behavior problems or large numbers of low achieving students. While transfers originally were occasioned by declining enrollment, court-ordered school desegregation has provided an additional impetus in recent years.

As a result of the *Morgan v. Hennigan* case in 1974, the claim was upheld that black students in Boston received a lower quality education than white students because of staffing and transfer policies.[19] Predominatly black schools were shown to be staffed with lower quality teachers and everchanging faculties. New, inexperienced teachers typically were assigned to these schools. As soon as they were eligible to transfer, they applied to leave. The "best" of these transfer teachers were selected by more desirable schools, leaving predominantly black schools with teachers no other school wanted. Because of *Morgan vs. Hennigan* and similar cases, teacher reassignment has become a component of many desegregation efforts. Experienced teachers, most of whom are white, have not reacted favorably to being reassigned to inner-city schools. Typically older, these teachers often fear for their personal safety. R.C. Newall reports that involuntary transfer is a major contributor to teacher stress.[20]

Besides the possible threats to personal safety, the inconvenience of learning new subjects, and the planning time required to teach multiple subjects, reassignments of any kind cause teachers to feel as if they do not control their professional destinies. Where school officials shuffle teachers around to satisfy the dictates of courts or the demands of economy and efficiency, teachers find it hard to regard teaching as *their* job. Depriving a worker of the right to determine how and where he can be most productive and subjecting him to the misuse of his talents constitute powerful incentives for seeking other employment.

Financial Insecurity

One of the most frequently heard reasons for the current failure of teaching to attract or retain talented teachers is the low salary. While I disagree with those who suggest that raising salaries dramatically is sufficient alone to correct the situation, greater remuneration clearly is one key component. It is difficult to lure competent teachers to work under increasingly adverse conditions when teacher salaries are falling behind the inflation rate and the salaries of other occupations.[21] What historian David Tyack terms teachers' "patient willingness to endure poverty" seems to be growing increasingly rare.[22]

Educational Research Service reported that the average of salaries paid classroom teachers increased 6.9 percent between 1977–1978 and 1978–79, while the Consumer Price Index rose 7.7 percent.[23] This means that the mythical average teacher in 1978–1979 earned $14,899. Two years later, when the National Education Association sampled its membership, it reported the average salary of respondents to be $17,209.[24] This figure represented a 43.3 percent increase since 1975–76, an impressive figure until one realizes that over the same period the Consumer Price Index rose 57.4 percent! The average starting salary of teachers in 1981–82 was $12,496, among the lowest for jobs requiring a college education.[25] Of additional concern was the averge maximum salary, which amounted to $24,472. That a veteran of 30 years in the classroom should take home less than

$25,000 seems a poignant reward for a lifetime of service to the young.

The National Center for Education Statistics projects only slight increases in teacher earning power during the eighties.[26] A review of expenditures for public education between 1919 and 1977, in fact, shows a steady decline in the percentage of school funds spent on instruction.[27] In 1919–20, 61 percent of school expenditures went to instruction. Fifty-eight years later the percentage had dipped to 55.8 percent and indications are it continues to drop.

Experienced teachers who are unable or unwilling to counteract rising financial insecurity by leaving teaching often are forced to "moonlight" at other jobs to make ends meet. Gene Barham is 45 years old, has two degrees, and 25 years teaching experience. At the top of his salary scale in suburban Richmond, Virginia, he earns $16,900. He is forced to work nights at a grocery store checkout counter. There are Gene Barhams in every city and suburb in the United States. Perhaps the plight of these individuals is best captured in the title of a high school teacher's "how to" book which appeared on shelves in 1978—*How to Teach School and Make a Living at the Same Time.*[28] The manual describes a variety of second jobs—from mail order schemes to home repair business—suited to the needs of hard-pressed teachers. Or possibly the most fitting last word comes from a Los Angeles teacher:

> The maximum salary for a beginning teacher in the Los
> Angeles Unified School District is a meager $1,348 per
> four–week pay period, $350 less than the pay for school
> painters, who are due for an increase. A family of four
> attempting to live on a starting teacher's salary easily qualifies
> for food stamps.

Why Johnny's Teacher Can't Teach

One major question which emerges from this chapter is whether Johnny's teacher will be allowed to do the job he entered teaching expecting to do. The signs are not encouraging. Will Johnny's teacher continue to tolerate the ambiguity which is teaching in return for steadily rising insecurity?

That the teacher's lot in the waning years of the twentieth century is ambiguity and insecurity seems to be firmly established. On the one hand, teachers hear that the job they have been doing is inadequate. On the other hand, they see that no agreement exists about how to remedy the situation. They cannot embark energetically on a new course of action because the options have not been thoroughly explored and the conditions constantly are being modified. Those who guide school systems cannot even agree on what the primary purpose of public education should be. Social control? Acquisition of basic skills? Pursuit of excellence? Cultivation of responsibility? Small wonder that teachers are confused and dismayed.

The situation can be likened to trying to hit a moving target. Each year seems to bring changes in the circumstances surrounding teaching. The changes frequently relate to what teachers are expected to accomplish. For example, during the seventies teachers were subjected to mandates concerning mainstreaming handicapped students, bilingual education, multicultural education, schooling for migrant children, equalization of academic and extra-curricular opportunities for female students, and the elimination of discriminatory practices in discipline. Teachers also were urged to teach reading in the content areas, provide counseling on drug and alcohol abuse, and report suspected cases of child abuse. The eighties have ushered in new expectations—greater stress on science, mathematics, and new technology, increased graduation requirements, the pursuit of academic excellence, and a shift from social studies back to history. In most instances, teachers receive little systematic preparation in college for these new responsibilities. The inservice training that sometimes accompanies new demands is perceived to be too little too late.

The unintended legacy of years of well-intentioned efforts to upgrade the quality of public schooling has been to demoralize teachers. The quality of public schooling has suffered because change agents and policymakers too frequently have ignored the needs of teachers. Critics of teachers unfairly have juxtaposed teacher needs against student needs, as if teacher needs could only be satisfied at the expense of student needs. It is hard to imagine, though, bringing about lasting improvements in public schooling without making life in classrooms better for *both* teachers and students. These issues are addressed in more detail in Chapter 7.

From time to time it has been necessary to remind critics that those who enter teaching swear no oath to martyrdom or masochism. They are human beings with the same needs as anyone else. They desire stability and security. They thrive on a reasonable challenge and a feeling of contributing to a better world. They need to be appreciated. They do not possess an infinite tolerance for innovation, no matter how well-intentioned. Like anyone else, they tend to regard suggestions about how they can do a better job as reprimands. They like to feel they control their destinies and influence the conditions under which they work.

When these human dimensions of teaching are overlooked, as they frequently have been, the result is the "objectification" of teachers.

In other words, teachers come to be treated like objects or pawns in a public service chess game. Sensing such treatment, teachers grow defensive and resistant to change.

Teacher objectification is but one of many factors which have contributed to making the job of teaching more difficult in recent years. Other factors mentioned in this chapter include the discrediting of traditional conceptions of teaching, uncertainty about the best way to conceptualize teaching, lack of financial incentives for teachers, and other forms of insecurity. These factors alone, however, cannot totally account for the present imperilment of the teaching profession. The fact that teachers do not exercise control over who they teach creates added difficulties for the profession. Chapter 4 looks at the changing nature of students and how these changes have placed greater strains on teachers.

What's Happened to Johnny?

Who is Johnny? He is the hypothetical "average American youngs-ter" immortalized by public school critics. *Why Johnny Can't Read.*[1] *Why Johnny Can't Add.*[2] *Why Johnny Can't Learn.*[3] *Why Johnny Burns His Schools Down.*[4] These recent book titles may soon be joined by *Why Johnny Can't Write, Why Johnny Can't Attend School,* and *Why Johnny Comes Marching Home* (Answer—he has been suspended from school!). Concern originally surfaced in the fifties when Johnny's academic progress was felt to be lagging behind Ivan's. Subsequently, worry over unsatisfactory achievement expanded to include other areas, such as discipline.

A talk with almost any teacher about the job of teaching leaves the impression that a major portion of contemporary educational difficulties stem from the nature of today's youth. Young people are perceived to have changed—for the worse. An N.E.A. "Teacher Opinion Poll" in 1980 indicated that 35 percent of all public school teachers are dissatisfied with their current jobs and that 41 percent would probably not become teachers if they had it to do over again.[5] Among the most frequently cited reasons for job dissatisfaction were student behavior and student attitudes toward learning. Apparently, non-teachers understand the sources of increasing strain for teachers. When asked to identify what they felt were the chief causes of teacher burnout and exit, a Gallup Poll sample selected discipline problems (63 percent) and lack of student motivation (37 percent) as the first and third most significant causes.[6] Low pay was the second most influential cause (52 percent).

It obviously is a mistake to argue that today's teachers are the first group of educators to confront serious student behavior problems. Truant officers were busy in 1881 as well as 1981.[7] One of the first psychology textbooks on adolescence devoted two chapters to cheat-ing.[8] Accounts of teachers' classroom experiences in early public schools reveal the fact that ensuring student attention was a constant challenge. Still, there is reason to believe that contemporary students are substantially less well-behaved than their predecessors. In other words, when teachers today consider leaving their profession because of student behavior, they are probably doing more than engaging in the time-honored exercise of one generation casting aspersions on the conduct of a succeeding generation.

Increasing problems are reported in a variety of areas, including lack of motivation, unreliability, dishonesty, disrespect for authority, and lawlessness. Before looking more closely at these concerns, however, it may be helpful to consider the social and demographic context in which they have arisen.

MORE WITH LESS

The social and demographic history of public education in the sixties and seventies is a chronicle of growing concentrations of students with less of what is required to benefit fully from public schooling. These students' lives often lack the stability so crucial to the development of aspirations and good habits. As the proportion of low achieving and unruly students in many schools increases, the capacity to retain and attract competent students diminishes. The deterioration of the quality of the student body accelerates, creating a constantly downward-moving spiral.

The origins of the downward spiral may be traced in part to the postwar "baby boom." Public schools in the late fifties began to stagger under the strain of unprecedented numbers of new students. In 1959, over 25 million students were enrolled in public schools in the United States.[9] A decade later enrollment had jumped to 36 million. The peak year for enrollments, 1970, found public schools accommodating nearly 46 million students. During this time additional teachers were hired and school buildings constructed, but overcrowding still existed and the adaptability of educators was constantly tested.

Not only was the school population growing, but its makeup was changing, creating unanticipated challenges for a predominantly white teacher workforce. In 1953 there were about 3½ million black and other minority students between the ages of 5 and 18.[10] In 1960 the figure had climbed to over 4½ million. Ten years later there were 7½ million minority students in the schools. Statistics for urban schools show a particularly dramatic increase, with some school systems shifting from predominantly white to more than 80 percent minority enrollment in the span of two decades.

Since the early sixties the ranks of minority students have expanded to include a growing percentage of recent immigrants, many of whom are not fluent in English. Vietnamese, Indochinese "boat people," Cubans, Haitians, and Mexicans are some of the largest groups. As in the past, public schools have been given the task of socializing these students. Unlike earlier times, however, schools also are expected to help preserve a sense of these students' native cultures.

Besides increasing numbers of minority and non-English-speaking students, conventional public schools have accommodated more exceptional and handicapped youngsters than ever before. Between 1953 and 1970 the number of individuals in special programs climbed from almost half a million to 3.2 million.[11] In 1980, the Census reported that 9.54 percent of the children between the ages of three and twenty–one were involved in special education.[12] Since the passage of PL 94–142 in 1975 most special education students have been placed ("mainstreamed") in regular classrooms for at least part of the school day.

The percentage of one kind of student has not been growing in many public schools, however. Gifted students are reportedly exiting for special public schools accessible by competitive examination, elite private schools, and parochial schools. The steady decline in nonpublic school enrollment which was recorded throughout most of the sixties shows signs of abating in many parts of the country. Private school enrollment rose from 366,157 to 722,318 in the late seventies, while public school numbers continued to drop.[13]

The gifted students who remain in public schools are perceived to be different from their predecessors by some teachers. Pamela Bardo, a stockbroker who left her teaching job in Los Angeles, expresses a frequently heard concern:

> My final disappointment came from an American studies team-teaching class where the school's best and brightest students turned in no more than half the assignments, all hastily prepared, and made independent study into social gatherings. I had taught the same class only three years before; a profound deterioration in student interest and participation between the earlier class and this one was readily apparent to me.[14]

The departure of many competent and gifted students together with a sharply declining birthrate among white, middle-class couples has produced a situation in which public schools in most cities expect to cater in the future primarily to nonwhite and working-class white students. These groups have a greater statistical likelihood of functioning below grade level and of being skeptical of the benefits of college preparatory programs.

In addition to changes in the number and nature of students served by public schools, changes have occurred in the domestic situations of many students. These changes transcend socioeconomic divisions.

As a result, teachers can no longer assume that their students come from stable homes or that they will remain in the same school system until graduation.

Between 1960 and 1972 the annual number of divorces increased by 80 percent to over 800,000.[15] By 1980 12 million school-age children or one-fifth of the school population was living with one parent.[16] The Bureau of the Census estimates almost half of the children born today will spend at least a year with one parent. Traditionally, single parents—typically mothers—lived with another relative who helped with child support and supervision.[17] In 1949, about half of single-parent families with children under six were headed by a relative other than the mother or father. This figure had dropped to 20 percent by 1973. Another example of what Keniston calls the "depopulation of the family" concerns unwed mothers. In 1960 one out of every twenty mothers was unmarried. By 1972, the figure had climbed to one in eight.[18] Changes of this magnitude have prompted observers like B. Frank Brown to maintain that the traditional American nuclear family—immortalized by television producers and patriotic interest groups—is more myth than reality.[19] Brown points out that only one family in seventeen conforms to the nuclear family "model"—salaried father, homemaking mother, children living with natural parents.

While not all students who live with one parent experience problems in school, they may do so more than peers from intact families. Reports from a study of 26 public schools indicate that children from one–parent families are more likely[20]

1. To get D's and F's in school.
2. To experience discipline problems such as truancy, referral, and alcohol and drug abuse.
3. To drop out of school.
4. To be absent from school.

Children from two-parent families may not escape all of the instability to which children living with one parent may be heir. In 1974, for the first time, more than half of all mothers of school-age children worked outside the home.[21] In a 1982 exposé entitled "Our Neglected Kids," *U.S. News and World Report* (August 9, 1982, p. 55) indicated that 5.2 million children thirteen and under are without supervision for significant parts of each day. The absence of a parent in the home when a child leaves for or returns from school can result in a lack of guidance and attention which may be related to youthful behavior problems and delinquency. Gangs of so-called "latchkey" adolescents from homes where both parents work have been implicated in after-school vandalism, arson, and other crimes.

Close contact between home and school is more difficult when a parent is unavailable during the school day.

The fact that more students in schools today have experienced considerable freedom from direct supervision at home means that they have grown accustomed to a degree of independence not often available at school. Many consequently find it difficult to conform to school rules and establish relationships with teachers. Add to this problem the fact that the growing number of young people from divorced parents are less likely to have available models of adults who can deal effectively with interpersonal problems and the personality makeup of today's student seems to have great potential for confrontations with teachers.

Besides problems derived from divorce and parent absence, young people today are subject to more transience and relocation. For example, between March 1970 and March 1971, almost 18 percent of the U.S. population—36,161,000—people relocated.[22] Rising transience has taken its toll on students and teachers. Since students are likely to experience a variety of schools before they graduate, educators find it more difficult to monitor student progress. Student files get lost. Curriculum continuity breaks down. A San Jose high school, and it is not atypical, reports more annual transfers in and out of the school than it has students enrolled.[23] Needless to say, orienting new students and checking out departing students is time-consuming, adding an extra burden to already busy schedules.

For their part, students faced with relocation must leave friends and trusted teachers. Activities and extra-curricular involvement have to be abandoned. Too much change of this kind can result in feelings of anomie and dislocation. It is understandable that high student turnover rates have been associated with greater numbers of behavior problems.[24]

Psychologist David Elkind has addressed a variety of issues related to contemporary youth in an important book entitled *The Hurried Child: Growing Up Too Fast Too Soon.*[25] He contends that a combination of factors—including the destabilization of homes, more time spent in self-care, media hype, and accelerating academic expectations—are creating a generation of young people who act increasingly like adults, but who lack emotional maturity and adult judgment. Elkind warns that these "hurried children" are subject to adult-type stress reactions and anger over having their emotional needs constantly subordinated to the needs of their parents. Such problems cannot help but manifest themselves in attitudes toward and performance in school.

The student bodies of a large number of schools today thus may lack many of the characteristics that traditionally have been associated with motivation to learn and cooperative behavior. The "critical mass" of competent students from stable homes in many schools is dwindling. More students are bringing to school serious learning, behavioral and emotional problems. The numbers of non–English-speakers and handicapped students are rising rapidly. Changes of these sorts were not expected by many of the people staffing today's schools. The contemporary student has created new challenges for these teachers, challenges for which they are not always trained nor prepared psychologically. The next section explores some of these challenges.

JOHNNY HAS CHANGED

Many adults—both educators and laymen alike—perceive that young people have changed. They are considered to be less motivated to work in school, less reliable, less honest, less respectful, and less law-abiding. When 300 veteran teachers and administrators in Minnesota were asked to comment on any changes they had observed in students over the years, they developed the following list:[26]

Students today are—
1. More assertive and outspoken
2. More oriented to instant gratification
3. More willing to challenge authority
4. Less fearful of adults

Critics of public education often concentrate so intensely on "proving" that deteriorating student conduct is attributable to poor teaching that they ignore the major demographic and social changes which have characterized recent years. In addition, they neglect the fact that, whatever their causes, student behavior problems exist. Their existence constitutes a source of serious disincentives for teachers and those anticipating careers in teaching.

Some scholars dispute the claim that young people are behaving worse than in past years. Walter Doyle, for example, contends that young people have misbehaved—to the consternation of their elders—for centuries.[27] Joan and Graeme Newman maintain that,

. . . a "crisis of discipline" has always existed in schools—or has existed at least since the Middle Ages, when the concept of childhood emerged and society came to regard children as constituting a group which was distinct from adults.[28]

Doyle goes further to argue that the only change in recent years has been the locus of youthful misbehavior. Today it tends to occur in school more than in the streets, a fact that he associates with greater enforcement of compulsory schooling laws.

Others argue that sufficient data do not exist to prove that students are behaving worse today then in the past.[29] They point out that parents and educators may *perceive* students are misbehaving more because they themselves are less capable of controlling misconduct or more skilled in detecting and reporting it.

Despite the difficulty of offering conclusive proof that Johnny is behaving worse than his parents or grandparents did when they attended school, I feel there is ample reason to believe that today's teachers confront behavior problems that differ both quantitatively and qualitatively from those faced by their predecessors.

Lack of Motivation

Students often seem to be unmotivated to work hard in school or to follow rules. This observation applies not only to those from working class backgrounds who plan to get jobs after graduation, but to many middle class, college–bound students as well. Lack of motivation is seen in private schools as well as public schools, helping to dispel the notion that students are the same as they have always been, only public schools have grown worse.[30]

It is a time when that which is deemed important is that which benefits the individual rather than the group or the society. Faulting adult society in general, journalist Dan Morgan, after talking with a random sample of 120 young people around the U.S., concluded,

> Never in the history of the United States has society given a generation so much and asked for so little in return. And many young people would respond: that is part of the problem.[31]

Whereas school once was widely regarded as the key to a better life for everyone, there is not a clear sense today that school "pays off" for the individual student.

Young people may, in part, be reflecting the disillusionment of their parents, who diligently pursued formal schooling only to discover that it did not yield security or salvation. Contemporary America is characterized by millions of seemingly successful adults who find little about which to exult. White-collar crime, divorce, mid-career crisis, stress, and loneliness are all manifestations of the adulthood awaiting today's youth.

Small wonder young people appear to be more hedonistic and less mindful of the "work ethic" than in the past. The future has lost much of its allure. Deferring gratification—like postponing major purchases during an era of double-digit inflation—does not necessarily make sense. When the future comes to be regarded more as a source of anxiety and uncertainty than of hope, the role of schools grows tenuous. Doing well in school loses much of its importance. In fact, when Jan Norman and Myron Harris surveyed 160,000 teenagers, they found that only 42 percent described school as necessary.[32] More than one in four felt school was boring.

The focus of youth's desire to achieve seems to have shifted from schoolwork to other targets, such as play. Christopher Lasch, in an articulate indictment of society's drift toward self-centeredness, points out that pleasure currently is defined as an end in itself.[33] The pursuit of pleasure, as a result takes on many of the properties of work. Young people begin to measure their achievement of pleasure—be it sexual conquests, drugs consumed, or days of school missed. What can be consumed assumes greater importance than what can be produced.[34]

Lack of motivation to work has spawned a new ethhic—if at first you don't succeed, quit. Students fail to elect difficult courses. The idea that success only results from diligence, discipline, and energy no longer is universally accepted. "Narcissistic entitlement," the feeling that things are owed a person without his doing anything to earn them, characterizes an increasing number of youth.[35] If school becomes too demanding, students simply drop out. It thus is no coincidence that the drop-out rate has been increasing recently, after decades of steady decline.

Given these developments, current teacher frustration becomes more understandable. Few teachers entered the profession expecting that a major portion of their work would entail convincing students of the value of schooling or cajoling them into doing what is expected of them. These tasks are particularly difficult with minority students, who frequently believe they have little chance of succeeding, even if they try hard.

Teachers, of course, have always contended with some students who were unmotivated to work or cooperate. In the past, however, it has been easier to remove these students from school. Changes in the laws governing school suspension and rising concern over abridgments of students' rights to an education have made it extremely difficult for educators to winnow unmotivated students. Unless these reluctant learners opt to drop out, they must be taught. Teachers resent having to devote time to students who are unlikely to benefit from instruction, while more motivated youngsters go unattended.

Unreliability and Dishonesty

If students are less motivated to work hard in school it is predictable that they will be less inclined to observe the ethical conventions traditionally associated with studentship. While accurate statistics are hard to obtain, reports from educators suggest that today's students may be less reliable and honest than their predecessors.

Behaviors teachers used to take for granted can no longer be assumed. Problems with tardiness and truancy have grown quite serious in many schools. Students often turn in falsified notes or relate bogus excuses to explain their absences. Dodging efforts by school personnel to ensure regular attendance constitutes a kind of game for many students. They realize that school personnel often are too overworked to follow-up every instance of possible illegal absence. The odds are that students will not be caught. Even if they are apprehended, the worst sanction schools typically impose is suspension—which may actually represent a reward to a chronic truant!

Unreliability and dishonesty are problems as well. Teachers complain that students fail to turn in assignments on time or sometimes at all. Even if work is completed, no assurance exists that students have done it themselves. Copying and plagiarism are widespread. When success does not come easily, students feel justified in using whatever means are necessary to get by. In their large survey of teenagers, Norman and Harris found that 55 percent reported cheating in school.[35]

To understand where students receive their cues, one need only look at the adult world. So much emphasis has been placed on ends that whatever means are utilized to get there seem acceptable. The process of acquiring skills and knowledge is less valued than the diploma awarded at the conclusion of the process. Cheating in college has become a national concern, as the West Point scandal indicated. Apparently the pressure to do well in college is so great that even good students will do whatever they can to maintain high grades. Sometimes these students resort to purchasing term papers, stealing needed books from the library, hiring students to take tests for them, and purposely giving fellow students erroneous information.

Problems concerning reliability and honesty extend to business and government as well. Absenteeism rates at large plants rival those at urban high schools—anywhere from 20 percent to 50 percent. Employees cannot be counted on to do the jobs expected of them. Reports of declining productivity in American industry abound. The Watergate and Abscam scandals indicate that even the highest levels of government are not immune to misconduct.

Noting the prevalence of unreliable and dishonest behavior in the adult world may make the phenomena more understandable, but it does little to ease the task of teaching. When students cannot be counted on to come to class regularly or complete assignments, teachers find it difficult to move steadily forward. They must constantly help absent students make up missed assignments, a process analogous to taking one step backward for every two steps forward. When students cheat on tests, copy homework, and plagiarize papers, teachers realize that students care less about learning than "getting by." Such a realization hardly inspires devotion to teaching.

Disrespect for Authority

For many teachers the most troublesome aspect of student misconduct today is the sense that students no longer respect their authority. Traditionally, behavior problems tended to derive from personal concerns or interpersonal frictions among students. Contemporary teachers, however, report many instances where the impetus for misconduct seems to be an unwillingness to submit to adult authority. Challenging teacher authority, in fact, has become a symbol of youthful pride in many areas. In other words, the route to peer respect is to defy adult authority. Part of the initiation rites of certain youth gangs in California involves going into a school and abusing a teacher or administrator.

Disrespect can manifest itself in a variety of ways. Students refuse to obey classroom and school rules. They fail to submit to punishments when charged with disobedience. Teachers are subjected to ridicule and name–calling, both within and outside of class. In a large study of student behavior problems commissioned by Congress, for example, researchers found that 48 percent of the teachers surveyed reported that students had insulted them or made obscene gestures at them in the preceding month.[37] Despite a decade's investment of time, training, expertise, and money, there is little indication that student behavior is less of a problem in the eighties than it was in 1970.[38]

The reasons for continuing reports of student disrespect are not hard to identify. Schools, after all, do not exist in isolation from society. The last two decades have been a time when authority at various levels has been questioned and challenged. The sixties blossomed with moves to decentralize decision-making and implement participatory democracy. Schools responded to these pressures by offering students more opportunities to participate in the governance process and make curricular choices. Many teachers tried to establish less formalized relations with students during this period.

While these developments succeeded in undermining the bases for traditional school authority, other developments intervened to prevent the emergence of more viable forms of authority. For one thing, the process of schooling, like the dollar, experienced considerable devaluation during the sixties. As the benefits of an education were perceived to decline, students had less to lose by challenging authority. Being suspended from school, for example, no longer struck fear in the hearts of many students.

Parents, perhaps unwittingly, abetted the growth of student disrespect by openly criticizing schools and educators. It is unlikely that a young person who hears his parents decry the low quality of instruction and defame teachers will continue to show much respect toward those who teach him. The situation can grow particularly tense when white teachers work with minority students. These students often reflect the frustrations and resentments that have built up in their parents as a result of years of trying to deal with the dominant culture. Teachers come to be perceived as symbols of the power structure that has oppressed minorities rather than individuals who can help disadvantaged youth escape poverty and oppression. They become easily accessible targets for deepseated anger—anger that might be more appropriately directed toward politicians, business leaders, and others who more directly chart the direction society takes.

Student disrespect also may have been unintentionally encouraged by student rights advocates. In the last two decades these individuals have pressed for extensive revisions in the laws pertaining to minors. Court cases have struck down a variety of school disciplinary practices, ranging from dress codes and prohibitions against free speech to suspensions without hearings. Many students are aware that teachers and administrators no longer enjoy the broad discretionary authority they once did. For their part, educators now live with the fear that a disciplinary action may result in an unpleasant confrontation with parents or a law suit. Lawyers, student advocates, and watchdog groups such as the Childrens' Defense League constantly are on the lookout for instances of discriminatory discipline and abridgements of students' constitutional rights.

Lawlessness

It is serious enough when students disregard with impunity classroom conventions and traditional norms governing relations with teachers. The increase in criminal conduct by students, however, has produced an even more alarming situation where the very physical safety of teachers is in jeopardy.

In 1980 the National Education Association polled its membership regarding attacks on teachers.[39] On the basis of the responses, it was estimated that 113,000 public school teachers were attacked during the preceding year. Of these, 2,500 were seriously injured. Attacks were not limited to urban schools, though most cases did occur in these places. While 11,000 teachers missed an average of five school days to recuperate from attacks, formal charges were filed in only 10 percent of the cases. The reason given most often by teachers for not pressing charges was fear of being regarded as a failure. In 25 percent of the cases, no disciplinary action at all was taken by the school against student assailants.

The dramatic increase in teacher victimization has contributed to a variety of psychological problems for teachers. The NEA Poll reports that one out of every four teachers worries about being physically attacked. The anxiety of never knowing when a confrontation might occur can take almost as great a toll as actually experiencing an attack. In his clinical contacts with Los Angeles teachers, psychiatrist Alfred Bloch reports that many manifest the symptoms of "combat neurosis." Block reports,

> In my experience treating teachers, certain aspects of working in inner–city schools appeared constant. Each teacher reported his environment was extremely stressful, and each believed that violence and vandalism were out of control on campus. Teachers indicted some school administrators for poor leadership, indifference,, and reluctance to discipline or expel disruptive or violent students. Apparently, these same administrators have also been reluctant to allow official reports of student assaults on teachers. In such an environment, school morale is poor; teachers are fearful and anxious about their physical survival. They often referred to their schools as "combat zones."[40]

Teachers must give more attention to protecting their property as well as their person. In the Safe School Study, 12 percent of the nation's 1.1 million secondary teachers reported having something stolen from them in a typical month.[41] About 6,000 teachers indicated that during the same time span they were likely to have something taken from them by force.

Students are directing their lawlessness at other students and school property as well as teachers. Theft was the most widespread of the offenses reported in the Safe School Study. About 2.4 million students had something stolen from them in a typical month. An estimated 1.3 percent of the nation's secondary students stated they were attacked during a one–month period, while one in five expressed fear they might be hurt or bothered at school.

Vandalism has become another major source of concern to educators. Estimates of the annual cost of vandalism to schools range from $50 million to $600 million.[42] Besides the destruction of property, schools are being subjected increasingly to burglaries, bomb threats, and false fire alarms. For all members of the school community—adults and students alike—the environment in which public education takes place is becoming less inviting.

While few would dispute the fact that lawless behavior in schools is not unique to the last few decades, there are strong indications that the frequency and severity of the problems has risen dramatically since the early sixties.[43] A California task force investigating school conflict and violence found compelling evidence of increased problems.[44] In 1970 a U. S. Senate Subcommittee on Juvenile Delinquency reported that incidents of vandalism in 110 school districts throughout the country climbed from 186,184 in 1964 to 250,549 in 1968.[45] School burglaries over the same period increased 86 percent.

Further support for the contention that the lawless behavior of youth has increased in recent years comes from statistics on juvenile delinquency. More crimes are being committed by youngsters under fifteen then adults over twenty–five.[46] In the last two decades juvenile crime has increased 1,600 percent.[47] Even allowing for improvements in the reporting of crime statistics, this figure is alarming. Rates of juvenile delinquency are climbing in small towns and suburbs as well as large cities, a further indication that changes in youthful behavior patterns are pervasive.[48]

Who Wants to Teach Johnny?

Traditionally, teaching offered little in the way of monetary remuneration or power. The work rarely ceased when school let out. The tasks of monitoring groups of students and maintaining a state of constant preparedness made teaching an exhausting enterprise. Still, no matter how difficult the job, there were always the students themselves. Eager minds. Childhood crushes. Awkward attempts to garner teacher favor. Funny incidents. Rites of passage.

Teachers today find fewer endearing qualities among their students. Yet policymakers often seem to have ignored this fact, preferring instead to act as if teachers invite mistreatment. Students *have* changed. Student behavior problems are nothing new to teachers, but their frequency and severity show definite signs of increasing. Even students who perform well in their school-work today often lack respect for teachers and fellow students. Students have become more like adults in many ways—in their assertiveness, disrespect, and independence. In other ways they are not so mature—unwilling to defer gratification and unable to comprehend the long–term benefits of schooling. As a result, working with young people today may no longer seem as intrinsically rewarding as it used to be. Teaching has come to be a matter of struggle and self-defense—both emotional and physical. Schools and classrooms no longer are havens from hostility. Much of the time that once was devoted to instruction and student advisement presently must go for control and discipline.

It is likely, of course, that some of the changes in student behavior and attitudes are traceable, at least in part, to inept or insensitive teaching. Teachers themselves are the first to admit that they make mistakes and that some members of their profession are generally ineffectual. To attribute rising rates of juvenile crime, campus disruption, truancy, unreliability, dishonesty, and apathy toward schooling solely to teachers, though, ignores the powerful influences on youth of parents, peers, the mass media, economics, and social norms. Also overlooked is the fact that students influence teacher behavior. Too often the process is described in unidirectional terms—with teachers always shaping student behavior. If some teachers today seem to manifest less dedication to teaching and diminished effectiveness, they possibly have been "conditioned" by contact with increasing numbers of difficult students.

While the precise etiology of changes in student behavior and attitudes may never be known, there is still the daily reality of working with students who do not see the value of formal schooling, are unwilling to work hard to obtain distant goals, and refuse to observe conventions of politeness and respect. It is a reality for which most teachers are unprepared. If policymakers expend all their efforts trying to determine who or what is to blame for youthful behavior problems and, by so doing, divert attention from the fact that teaching—particularly in urban areas—is becoming less rewarding materially and intrinsically, they may be ensuring that future students will not have access to able and committed instructors.

CHAPTER 5

Complaints and Constraints— The Societal Context of Teaching

Teaching takes place in schools, but schools do not exist in isolation. They are fundamental elements of communities. How teachers feel about their work cannot be separated from how teachers feel they are perceived by community members. Today teachers frequently feel as if they were the closest and most convenient targets for public discontent. Local citizens may be outraged by federal mismanagement, state government spoils systems, or the salary of the school Superintendent, but when they take aim, they may only be able to reach the nearest teacher. As a result, policymakers have difficulty separating public criticism meant for teachers from public criticism intended for other targets. One thing is clear, however. Most teachers enter the profession hoping to help others, not to be regarded as a prime source of public concern.

While it is true that teachers periodically have confronted public complaints since the inception of the common school, they have rarely encountered such pervasive and well-documented criticism. In addition, critics in the past have not been so willing or anxious to back up their rhetoric with demands for formal constraints on teacher behavior, including performance standards, codes of conduct, and provisions for greater citizen involvement in educational decision making. In short, the relationship today between teachers and the public can hardly be characterized by an abundance of trust and good will.

TARGETS FOR BLAME

There is a lot about American society in the last decades of the twentieth century that merits concern. Double-digit inflation threatens to erode the quality of life Americans once boasted was the best in the world. Unemployment is high, particularly among young, minority males. Crime and disorder abound. Cities go bankrupt. Amer-

58

ican industry watches as foreign competitors make inroads into once secure markets. Minorities complain that de facto segregation and racism are erasing the civil rights gains of the sixties.

While the problems are cause for alarm, it is also alarming to note the ease with which many social critics and policymakers lay them at the schoolyard gate. Teachers have the sometimes dubious distinction of being the symbol of the public school. When student achievement declines, it is the teacher who has failed to teach basic skills. When unemployment and juvenile delinquency climbs, it is the teacher who has neglected career education, good work habits, and student self-esteem. Low teacher expectations for minority students are regarded as a subtle form of racism. Lack of classroom control and teacher reluctance to model appropriate behavior are cited as reasons why young people lack discipline and respect for authority. The waste of public resources on questionable educational innovations and teacher pressure—through collective bargaining—for higher salaries are cited as contributors to fiscal crisis. Taxpayers cannot understand why education costs skyrocket while enrollments decline.

Why is the teaching profession seemingly more vulnerable to criticism than in the past? The reason is not that today's teachers simply are less competent than their predecessors. In preceding chapters I have argued that the nature of teachers' work and of the students with whom they deal have changed. There have been other changes as well—in the nature of the citizenry and its attitudes toward public education.

Public education in the United States once enjoyed the status of a secular religion. No official, state-sanctioned religion, of course, was permitted. Public education filled the void, however. Through lay priests—teachers—the schools imparted expectations, norms, and a sense of how the world functioned. Schools promised salvation in the form of a productive adult life. In order to achieve this "promised land," students expected to work hard and obey authority.

Public education does not inspire the reverence and respect it once did. Ironically, teachers are partially to blame for this situation. They did their job too well! By educating the vast majority of the nation's youth, American teachers helped create a situation in which public schooling ceased to be a special or privileged experience. Between 1960 and 1970, for example, there was approximately a 39 per cent increase in the percentage of adults in the United States with a college degree.[1] The public began to take literacy for granted. It could be imagined that a comparable devaluation of Christianity might occur if people believed that everyone entered heaven.

Not only have most Americans since World War II gone to high school, but many have also attended college. As a result, teachers no longer can boast that they have more years of schooling than the parents of many of their students. It is not uncommon for teachers to deal with parents who feel—rightly or wrongly—that they are more knowledgeable.

That the quality and value of teachers and schooling have been subjected to increasing criticism in recent years is not to say, however, that the public has entirely given up on public education. Indicative of the public's ambivalent attitude toward schools is the fact that in the same breath that educators are blamed for various social ills they are called on to correct them. In other words, many citizens still see schools as primary agents for the betterment of society. Thus, a national commission investigating the causes of racial violence in the mid-sixties indicts schools for perpetuating racism and inequality and then recommends that federal support be provided for school-based efforts to increase the likelihood that minority youth will obtain worthwhile employment.[2]

Critical of schools and those who work in them, yet unwilling to completely abandon public education as a panacea for social ills, Americans increasingly have sought ways to constrain the conduct of educators and make them more directly accountable for their actions. That more constraints might demoralize teachers and actually diminish their effectiveness does not seem to have occurred to many proponents of greater regulation.

Arthur Wise has written perceptively of the growing campaign to regulate education—a move he links to the desire of those outside the traditional decision-making structure of public education to influence schools. Educational policymakers have been slow to delineate the extent to which these other policymakers should be involved in technical decisions. Wise warns that the regulatory trend may have some negative impact and points to a process he labels hyperrationalization. Manifestations of hyperrationalization include excessive prescription, procedural complexity, and first-order solutions:

> *Excessive prescription.* Policymakers have several means of influencing a school system. They may prescribe the inputs to the system, the process the system is to employ or the outcomes the system is to achieve. Traditionally, policymakers restricted themselves to prescribing inputs such as the minimum expenditure, the required number of days of school and the minimum qualifications of teachers. Recently policymakers have begun to prescribe expected outcomes like reading level, functional literacy and citizenship skills. . . .

Often an outcome prescription is made without considering whether it is attainable given resource (or input) constraints. Numerous logical and practical inconsistencies are the likely result of efforts to prescribe input, process, and outcome controls.

Procedural complexity. Procedural complexity is often the result of efforts to respond to demands for sharing power. It results when those in power wish to appear to share authority without, in fact, surrendering authority. The responses is a procedural rather than a substantive change. . . .

First-order solution. A school problem is identified and the statement of the problem becomes the statement of the solution as a first-order analysis of the problem is made to yield the solution. Schools are not accountable, so create an accountability programme. High school graduates are incompetent, so create a competency-based high school graduation programme. Teachers are incompetent, so create a competency-based teacher education programme. The creation of a programme with the same name as the problem of yields the appearance of coping with the problem, if at all, at the very core of the education enterprise. Tinkering in superficial ways with outcomes of schooling is very far from the real solution.[3]

Hyperrationalization of educational policy can be attributed to at least three developments—greater court involvement in education, the accountability movement, and shifts in educational finance. Each of these derives, in large part, from changing attitudes toward public education by the public and its elected and appointed officials.

Legal Constraints

During the past quarter century teachers have been affected by court decisions in three broad areas: student rights, equity, and professional malpractice. The collective impact of these decisions has been to inhibit teacher discretion. Many teachers also perceive that their ability to control students has been undermined.

Decisions regarding student rights are illustrative. Beginning with *Tinker v. Des Moines* in 1969, a series of court actions established the principle that students do not shed their constitutional rights "at the schoolhouse door." Students have been guaranteed the right to free speech—both verbal and symbolic (as in the wearing of an armband). Their publications may not be censored, and their dress may not be regulated, except under certain conditions. Students may be given access to their official records and have the right to challenge any entries. In matters involving suspension, students must be accorded due process rights, including an official notification of charges and a hearing. Punishments such as lengthy suspensions and expulsions have been challenged successfully because they deny students access to an education, thus depriving them of their rights under the Fourteenth Amendment.

Backed by recent legislation, a special category of court decisions related to student rights and the Fourteenth Amendment concerns equality of educational opportunity for special groups of students. In an attempt to establish greater equity, the courts have ordered the busing of students to achieve racial balance, inclusion of pregnant and married students in regular school activities, and cessation of discriminating practices based on sex, handicap, or native language. Teachers may even be transferred in order to integrate faculties and thereby increase the likelihood of equal opportunity for students.

Few would fault the spirit guiding court decisions and legislation protecting the rights of students. Where teachers grow concerned, however, is in the execution of the laws. In schools beset by chronic student misconduct, according students their due process rights and completing the paperwork required by various regulations may tax personnel, retarding their ability to maintain a reasonable degree of order. When dismissed students who have behaved in a blatantly disrespectful or dangerous way are reinstated because of procedural technicalities, teachers fear reprisals and worry about classroom control. Teachers also are concerned that overemphasis on student rights may undermine respect for authority and encourage students to challenge any teacher action.

The increase in malpractice cases and the proliferation of legal guides for educators suggests that teachers' concern over challenges to their authority is justified. A student who feels he has been unreasonably punished may either institute a criminal action against a teacher or sue for damages in a civil action. Teachers are subject to sanction not only by the courts but by educational agencies as well. Individuals who become involved in litigation may also find themselves subjected to a hearing before a local school board or a State Department of Education tribunal.

Among the sanctions available to educational agencies are suspension from teaching duties, dismissal, and revocation of the teaching certificate. In a controversial New York City case in 1980, the Chancellor of the school system even attempted to prevent a teacher indicted by a grand jury for obscenity from collecting his pension benefits. This case was noteworthy because of the reasoning used by an investigation panel in reaching its verdict. The panel's argument seemed to place teachers in a position where they must be subject not only to the laws and regulations of the state, but to the possibly arbitrary norms of the community:

> A person who accepts a teaching position willingly places himself and his conduct in the arena of public attention. What may be acceptable in other walks of life takes on an entirely different aspect when engaged in by a teacher. A teacher accepts a special place within the community. . . . A teacher is a role model for students to emulate. . . .
>
> Both the teacher's private life and public life are the sum total of that person. One does not exist in the absence or exclusion of the other. . . .[4]

Such reasoning would appear to uphold the right of community groups to dismiss teachers who act in any manner deemed contrary to community norms. Conceivably, teachers may even be removed because of their beliefs. Thus, a teacher who supports abortion in an antiabortion community might be challenged as an inappropriate role model. To date the courts have not spoken in a definitive way to the issue of how much of a teacher's constitutional rights may be abridged by a community striving to protect its belief system. Until they do, it would appear that many teachers must live with the disturbing possibility that they are not as free as other citizens.

The recent wave of efforts to censor the books teachers use in school testifies to the willingness of communities—or segments of communities—to intervene in the professional lives of teachers. Judith Krug of the American Library Association estimated that between 1975 and 1980 three times as many censorship attempts were made as in the preceding decade.[5] An effort is also being mounted to give legislative support to those who would deny academic freedom in the name of community values. In 1979 Senator Paul Laxalt (R-Nevada) introduced the Family Protection Act. Supported by ultraconservatives who normally oppose federal intervention, the bill would have prohibited:

1. Teaching any course "seeking to inculcate values or modes of behavior which contradict the demonstrated belief and values of the community."
2. Use of any educational materials that would "tend" to denigrate, diminish, or deny the role differences between the sexes as it [sic] has been historically understood in the United States.

The bill also supported school prayer and private education and attacked equal opportunity for young women in athletics and the nondiscrimination requirement for federal aid recipients. What the Laxalt bill did not do, however, was clearly define what constitutes a "community." As a result no assurance exists that teachers would not be vulnerable to challenge by highly vocal special interest groups, such as the Moral Majority, that claim they speak for the community.

The Accountability Movement

The Laxalt bill suggested the lengths to which portions of the public and their representatives will go to place constraints on teachers and schools. Under the name of accountability, efforts have been made in the last decade to legislate school effectiveness and circumscribe professional practice through a steadily growing number of regulations. The regulations apply to every phase of schooling—input, throughput, and output. Use of terms from the business world are not inappropriate here, since much of the impetus behind the current wave of educational regulations seems to derive from concern over issues like efficiency, economy, and productivity. Taken individually, these accountability measures often are sensible and receive teacher support. Collectively, however, they seem overwhelming—a vast array of new requirements creating the impression that *all* teachers, rather than a troubled minority, need strict supervision.

Attempts to ensure quality education at the input phase generally have involved greater state supervision of teacher training and more rigorous assessment of teacher candidates. State agencies concerned with teacher certification are placing more pressure on Schools of Education to exercise greater quality control over who has access to training in education. Training programs themselves have also been subjected to regulation. State Departments of Education are insisting that teachers take certain courses in order to be eligible for certification. Requirements range from classroom management and cultural awareness to remedial reading and mainstreaming the handicapped learner. A number of states now require teacher training to be "competency-based."[6]

To assess the extent to which the training is successful, states also are mandating proficiency tests for teacher candidates. Some states, mostly in the South, require norm-referenced tests such as the National Teacher Examination. Other states, like California, are exploring the use of tests to certify that teachers can read, write, and calculate sufficiently well to serve as good models for students. Federal courts, however, have struck down minimum cut-off score requirements on such tests as the National Teachers Examination and the Graduate Record Examination on the ground that performance on the tests was not substantially related to job requirements.[7]

Despite recent events the idea of teacher testing is not new. The National Teacher Examination was developed in 1940. In other words, there is historical evidence to indicate that testing alone will not ensure quality instruction. As a result, efforts have been made to increase the regulation of the throughout phase—or what teachers do in schools to try to achieve student outcomes. Teacher evaluation is a key component to the throughout monitoring process, and legislation such as California's Stull Bill require all teachers to be evaluated periodically. In 1981, North Carolina became the first state to mandate a systematic statewide means of appraising teachers that includes specific standards of performance.[8] *In Harrah (Oklahoma) Independent School District v. Mary Jane Martin* (1979), the Supreme Court of the United States upheld the right of school boards to fire tenured teachers who refuse to comply with continuing education requirements.[9] At least 28 states require or are considering requiring some form of inservice training for teachers.[10] More pressure is being placed on administrators to remove incompetent teachers and ensure quality instruction. Oregon, for example, expects its Superintendents to submit to an annual public evaluation of their effectiveness and, ultimately, the effectiveness of the employees under their jurisdiction.

In 1981 New Jersey went a step beyond mandatory teacher and administrator evaluation to introduce legislation that would establish a merit pay system. Such a scheme presumably would build greater accountability into teaching by rewarding the individuals who demonstrate the most success with students. Teacher groups traditionally have opposed merit pay on the grounds that it encourages competition between teachers for more able students and easier assignments.

In the same spirit as merit pay are performance-based teacher layoffs. As school enrollments decline and money for education becomes more scarce, school systems are forced to let teachers go. Seniority typically has guided layoff decisions. Recently, however, some school systems have begun to use performance criteria to determine which teachers stay and which teachers go. While the practice may seem reasonable in theory, Susan Johnson conducted a study of four districts and found a number of practical problems with performance-based layoffs. Though principals reported having little difficulty identifying poor teachers, they admitted that few poor teachers remained in their schools. When it came to making performance distinctions between average and above average teachers, principals were much less confident in the validity of their judgments. Johnson also speculated that establishment of performance-based layoffs as a longterm policy could further undermine labor-management relations and community respect for schools. In conclusion, she observed:

> Little is understood about what holds a school together and makes it feel like a good place to learn, yet one might guess that the answer is somehow tied up in the informal, cooperative relationships between principal and teacher, teacher and teacher, and ultimately between teacher and student. The legal standards for procedural fairness require a rationalized approach to teachers and their work. But the workself is not rationalized . . . Sorting, scoring, and ranking performance objectifies the relationship between teachers and administrators. . . .
>
> In an institution that, at its best, promotes acceptance and inclusion, performance-based layoffs introduce competition and exclusion.[11]

Besides evaluation strategies aimed at upgrading the quality of instruction, a plethora of regulations pertaining to what teachers do have appeared during the last decade. These regulations range from required procedures for ordering textbooks to mandates on how to deal with minority, handicapped, and female students. In areas with large non-English-speaking populations, teachers are pressed to develop second language competence. Secondary school teachers are expected to acquire proficiency in teaching basic skills. Regulations govern the handling of disciplinary cases, reporting of drug use and child abuse, and what can be included in student records. An example of how regulated the daily lives of some teachers have become is contained in an informational letter required by federal and state law to be mailed annually to parents of Palo Alto, California, students. Among the areas subject to regulation are the following:

1. Option to withdraw from health instruction that conflicts with moral or religious beliefs.
2. Parent notification if discussion of human reproductive organs or their functions is to occur in class.
3. Procedures for administering prescribed medication in school.
4. Reporting procedures for attendance and absence.
5. Provision of alternative schools and programs.
6. Pupil records and release of information.
7. Corporal punishment.
8. Suspension and expulsion.
9. Discrimination and affirmative action.

The problem is not necessarily that any particular regulation is offensive to teachers. The real issue concerns the capacity of teachers to remember all of the regulations, comply with them consistently,

and complete the paperwork associated with them while still performing their normal instructional duties. When teachers must take
time away from teaching to deal with regulations, questions can be
raised about how much the regulations contribute to better learning.

Since regulating the input and throughput phases of education
have not always produced the results sought by the public, attempts
have also been made to control outputs—namely the students themselves. All states in one way or another regulate the subjects required
of students seeking a high school diploma. Thirty-eight states require
some form of minimum competency test for students (Dearman and
Plisko, 1980). The tests typically are administered at several points
in a student's schooling to ascertain if he has fulfilled expectations
in basic skills. Eighteen states use competency tests to determine if
students can graduate from high school. While few teachers question
the reasoning behind these quality control measures, they acknowledge that the presence of externally developed tests decreases their
curricular flexibility and makes it more difficult to include subject
matter relevant to certain groups of students. There is also the fear
that too much stress on "minimum" standards may result in the
minimum becoming the maximum.

Retrenchment

While the impact on teachers' lives of legal constraints and legislative regulations has been substantial, it may appear relatively
minor in comparison to the changes being wrought by economic
retrenchment. As a result of a variety of forces, including declining
enrollments, sustained inflation, and taxpayers' revolts, school systems
are finding it difficult to deliver basic services or maintain required
programs. As the birthrate declines and the number of couples without
children and senior citizens with grown children increases, the percentage of taxpayers with a direct stake in the public schools drops.

Oregon provides an interesting case study. In 1982, voters narrowly
rejected Ballot Measure 3, an initiative that would have rolled property
taxes back to 1979 levels, limited annual tax increases to 1.5 percent
of assessed valuation, and reduced local school budgets by up to 50
percent. Supporters of the initiative defined education as a "non-
essential" service, while police and fire protection were classified as
essential. Such a move was possible because in areas where large
numbers of voters were concentrated, like Portland, fewer than one
adult in five had a child in the public schools.[12]

Politicians know their demographics. They admit that funding for
education is no longer a "sacred" issue. Teachers may not have
expected to have to behave politically when they selected their career,

but today they have little choice but to lobby and compete for diminishing resources with other interest groups. In 1978 California became the first state in recent times to limit the ability of localities to raise revenue for education and other public services from property taxes. Idaho and Massachusetts have followed suit. The number of school budgets and bond issues that go down to defeat has increased dramatically in recent years. In 1981 in Oregon, for example, 59 percent of the local school budgets failed.[13]

On a national basis, table 3 gives an indication of the downward trend in approved bond issues over a sixteen-year period.

The growing mood of austerity has affected teachers in a number of ways. Job insecurity has previously been noted. Financially strapped school systems are forced to eliminate programs and positions. In many urban school systems all but the most senior teachers do not know from one year to the next if they will still have a job. Because contracts typically require that teachers receive advance warning if their jobs may be terminated, spring has become the season of the "pink slip." Some districts routinely send job termination warnings to all teachers. As previously noted, the impact on a veteran teacher of receiving such a notice can be devastating. Teachers report feeling devalued and anxious. Even if the fall finds their job preserved for another year, they have no guarantee they will be teaching what they want or where they want. It was common in California following Proposition 13 to find elementary teachers teaching high school mathematics, counselors teaching physical education, and suburban teachers working in inner city schools.

Table 3. Results of Public School Bond Elections[14] 1961–1962 to 1976–77

Fiscal Year	Total elections	Number Approved	Percent Approved
1961–62	1,432	1,034	72.2
1962–63	2,048	1,482	72.4
1963–64	2,071	1,501	72.5
1964–65	2.041	1,525	74.7
1965–66	1,745	1,265	72.5
1966–67	1,625	1,082	66.6
1967–68	1,750	1,183	67.6
1968–69	1,341	762	56.8
1969–70	1,216	647	53.2
1970–71	1,086	507	46.7
1971–72	1,153	542	47.0
1972–73	1,273	719	56.5
1973–74	1,386	779	56.2
1974–75	929	430	46.3
1975–76	770	391	50.8
1976–77	858	477	55.6

In addition to job insecurity and dislocation, retrenchment has meant teachers' earnings—never very high—have failed to keep pace with inflation. Distressed districts not only have eliminated regular raises based on years of experience and training, but cost-of-living increases as well. In hard-hit states like Michigan and Oregon, teacher unions have been compelled to renegotiate contracts and accept less pay. Cuts in extracurricular programs reduce the opportunities for teachers to earn extra money supervising student activities. Sabbatical leaves have been suspended by many districts.

The impact of retrenchment on earnings and job security is bad enough, but evidence exists that working conditions are adversely affected as well. These changes can be appreciated by using the analogy of a steadily declining spiral. Teachers in school systems facing annual budget cuts seem locked in a situation where each budget cut sets in motion forces that help to accelerate worsening job conditions.

Consider, for example, the case of San Jose High School—neither the school least nor most adversely affected by declining enrollment and Proposition 13 in California.[15] Located in downtown San Jose, the high school has experienced changes in the makeup of its student body over the past decade. When retrenchment began, San Jose High was serving a population predominantly composed of Mexican-Americans, Portuguese, Blacks, and Indochinese immigrants. Most of the 1400 students came from low socioeconomic status families.

In the fall of 1979 San Jose High learned that one-sixth of its teaching staff—fourteen teachers—did not have jobs. The school day was reduced from six to five periods, and 44 periods of instruction were lost, mainly in such areas as remedial reading, industrial arts, and English-as-a-Second Language. To preserve their jobs, many of the teachers who remained had to agree to teach subjects for which they were not trained.[16] Twenty paraprofessionals, all five counselors, an attendance clerk, and several campus supervisors were also released. The budget for extracurricular activities was cut, resulting in the reduction of the athletic program by half and elimination of band and dramatics.

Because of these cuts, the workload for most San Jose High teachers increased substantially. Average class size rose from 23 to 31 students. Fewer resources were available for materials, and most of the paraprofessionals whose presence allowed teachers to spend more time working with individual students were gone. The new five-period day meant teachers no longer had a planning period. Cuts at the administrative level forced teachers to handle all but the most serious of their discipline problems.

Teachers thus found they had less time and fewer resources to work with larger numbers of students. Students received less attention and supervision. They grew more restless, and acts of disruption and disrespect increased. Behavior problems required more teacher intervention, further reducing the time available for direct instruction. With less instructional time, student achievement began to drop, leading to greater student dissatisfaction and even more classroom management problems. In this manner, the downward spiral was set in motion at San Jose High.

Problems were exacerbated by the fact that more able students were withdrawn by their parents and placed in suburban or private schools. In some cases parents actually falsified addresses or used addresses of relatives to effect transfers. For San Jose High teachers, the departure of high ability students meant working with larger concentrations of lower ability students. Public expectations did not change to reflect these changing working conditions, however. Many in the community seemed to expect teachers to achieve greater results with fewer resources!

Eventually assistance was found for San Jose High. A campaign to publicize conditions at the school resulted in a wave of community support, pressure on the Board of Education, and eventual reinstatement of some teaching positions. Teachers, however, hardly could afford a sigh of relief. No sooner does one crisis pass then another one surfaces. Since 1979, each year has brought the threat of a new round of budget-cutting, reductions in force, and belt-tightening. In 1980 an initiative to limit the state's ability to "bailout" local districts (through the use of state income taxes) was placed before the voters. Proposition 9 was defeated, but it contributed to perpetuating a climate of uncertainty—hardly an atmosphere conducive to long-range planning, professional commitment, or enthusiasm. In the summer of 1983, no longer able to ensure adequate resources for its schools, the San Jose Unified School District took the unprecedented legal action of applying for bankruptcy. This drastic action resulted from the district's inability to honor a court order to provide teachers with a negotiated retroactive pay increase.

San Jose High's experience may not be unusual, either. Studies elsewhere suggest that retrenchment is causing professional and personal problems for many teachers. One study of three New York City high schools affected by budget cuts in 1975 reported a host of disturbing byproducts of cutbacks, including deteriorating relations between teachers and teacher burnout.[17] Scarce resources occasioned greater competition among teachers. Students became commodities in this process, with white and bright students valued for their motivation and handicapped students valued for the extra funds they brought to the school. Teachers with smaller classes, greater numbers of bright students, or newer textbooks encountered claims of favoritism from colleagues straining to instruct classes of 30 to 45 less able students with outdated materials or no materials at all.

Many New York City teachers frankly admitted not knowing how much longer they could keep up the pace. Each year they report working harder to accomplish what they did the previous year. Each year they confront larger numbers of lower-ability, less-cooperative students with fewer resources and less certainty concerning where, when, what, and if they will teach the following year. These teachers are caught in a double bind. If they try to compensate for lost resources by working harder, they not only risk physical and psychological exhaustion, they help confirm the public's perception that schools can get by with less money. If the teachers continue to teach, but accept the fact they cannot meet the needs of all their students, they must watch more students fall behind.

Worst of all, the strategies these New York City teachers were compelled to use to help them cope in the short-run with growing class sizes and diminishing resources seem likely to foster more serious problems later on. For instance, teachers cut back on tests and assigned fewer essays and written exercises because they lacked sufficient time to grade them. Less homework was given because teachers could not let students take textbooks home for fear that the books would not be replaced if lost. Over time, of course, such pragmatic strategies will tend to effect student learning adversely, thus increasing teacher workload even more.

An Ethos Hostile to Professionalism

Public criticism certainly is nothing new to teaching, but when complaints lead to fewer resources for education at the same time that expectations and regulations increase, the profession must find itself in a precarious position. The very notions on which professionalism is based are challenged when teachers no longer can be reasonably sure they will have the opportunity to teach what they were trained to teach or where they feel they can be most effective. Teachers today confront a variety of mixed messages from the public. They are told to use fewer resources to raise the achievement of students who increasingly question the value of an education. The task is particularly difficult when more able students are placed in nonpublic schools. The public also expects teachers to be in greater control of students, but it refuses to allow teachers greater authority over schooling.[18] In the unenviable position of being both civil servants and professionals, teachers are expected to treat all clients the same and every client as an individual.

It is not surprising that under such circumstances teachers begin to find their occupation unsatisfying. As indicated in Chapter 1, Sarason finds that teachers are not the only professionals currently rethinking their choice of career.[19] He attributes rampant disillusionment, in part, to the fact that greater numbers of professionals are spending their working lives in organizations. The values which guide the operation of these organizations tend to be efficiency, economy, and productivity. To read modern organization literature or hear executives speak, it would appear that there are no other values worth considering. It is easy for pressured policymakers to forget that the democratic principles upon which the nation was founded did not include efficiency, economy, or productivity. Instead, values such as justice for all and citizen involvement were championed. While autocracy or dictatorship may, under certain conditions, function more efficiently than democracy, few would urge a change in government. Perhaps "helping" professions such as teaching deserve to be judged using criteria other than those of private industry. More concerning these matters will be said in the concluding chapter.

Another part of the problem teachers face derives from the society itself, rather than the nature of its organizations. At present, the future seems to have lost its allure. After decades of worshipping the notion of progress, many are beginning to wonder if life in the future will be better than it is today. Continuing inflation, decreasing natural resources, and worldwide unrest point to a steadily eroding quality of life. Skepticism about the future is manifested in a number of ways, including the reluctance of many people to have children. The prevailing ethic is becoming hedonism—making the most of the present. Since the idea of schooling is closely associated with faith in the future, any era when the future ceases to be attractive is one in which schools and those who work in them are likely to be in trouble.

Educators now find themselves competing for resources with a variety of other interest groups. Senior citizens—who make up a growing percentage of the population—seek to protect their fixed incomes and resist efforts to raise additional revenues for schools. Middle-class immigrants to suburbia and families that can afford private education resent having to contribute to public schools in urban areas. Proposed voucher schemes and tax credit plans promise tax relief for those who opt for nonpublic schools. A California politician who preferred to remain anonymous summed up the plight of teachers well when he said, "Today, education is bad politics."

That the profession is in trouble should now be clear. The reasons are complex and encompass changes in the nature of the job of teaching, the societal context in which it takes place, and the clients themselves. The next section explores problems in the support systems available to teachers.

Part III

Teachers in Search of Assistance

CHAPTER 6

How Helpful is Higher Education?

Time was when the relationship between higher education and the public schools could be characterized by a type of benign paternalism. Noted education scholars like Elwood Cubberley wrote glowing accounts of the schools. The American educational system was heralded as one of the nation's greatest achievements and held up as a model to the rest of the world. When criticism was heard from the laity, champions of public education rose from the ranks of college faculties. Protective of the schools and their employees, professors and college presidents challenged the critics to find a better, more equitable system.

To say that times have changed risks understatement. In Chapter 2 it was noted, for instance, that colleges and universities are openly criticizing high schools for failing to adequately prepare students for the rigors of higher education. Noted officials from Derek Bok of Harvard to Donald Kennedy of Stanford call for greater emphasis on academic excellence in public education. Faced with diminishing public revenues, institutions of higher education vie openly with elementary and secondary schools for resources.

Traditionally colleges and universities have provided three basic types of service to schools. First, they prepared prospective teachers for certification. Second, they offered advanced training and inservice opportunities to experienced teachers. Third, they offered technical assistance to schools in the form of research, development, and consultation.

Thus, it is not surprising that teachers and policymakers might look to higher education for assistance with some of the contemporary problems with teaching identified in previous chapters. When teachers, however, seek help from colleges, universities, and R & D centers—either collectively or as individuals, they are apt to confront some of the very problems that characterize their work environments. Teacher needs, for example, must be funnelled through bureaucratic channels and weighed against competing concerns. Colleges, universities, and R & D centers, like public school systems, are big organizations. So, too, are other sources of assistance for teachers—federal and state education agencies, professional groups, private foundations, and even teacher unions. These will be discussed in later chapters.

The irony, then, for today's teachers is that in the very act of enlisting help to improve working conditions they are likely to encounter some of the problems they are trying to ameliorate—red-tape, ambiguity, unresponsive officials, insensitive policies, devaluation of professional judgment, and so on. It is this dimension of the job of teaching that Sarason failed to note in his otherwise very thorough treatment of the pitfalls of being a professional. It is disillusioning enough to confront such unexpected features of teaching as lack of discretion and influence without encountering the same problems when dealing with support services.

Preservice Education

The first contact with higher education for most teachers comes when they are undergraduates preparing for teaching. Teacher education is a big business. It is available at nearly 1,400 colleges and universities in the United States.[1] Teacher training frequently pays the bills for costly doctoral programs at many institutions. By assigning prospective teachers to large lecture classes staffed by teaching assistants, adjunct professors, and non-tenured faculty members, universities are able to offer their doctoral students small seminars taught by respected senior professors.

The economic dimension of teacher education cannot be over-emphasized. Timothy Weaver, for example, attributes many of the current problems with the quality of teacher education to the selfishness of institutions of higher education during the seventies when enrollments declined. He contends that,

> cumulative decisions of institutions, acting individually, in self interest, to gain a greater share of the shrinking market, had the effect of throwing gasoline on a fire. Institutions reacted to declining applications like the plague. They intensified efforts to recruit and retain students, and at the same time relaxed standards in order to capture more of those who did apply.[2]

Since Lexington Normal School opened its doors in 1839 in Massachusetts, the "business' of preparing public school teachers has been the focus of much uneasiness and debate. When policymakers have worried about the quality of public education, they typically have turned to teacher educators with their charges. Concern has been voiced over what trainees are and are not taught, how they are taught, and by whom they are taught. A sampling of recent criticism is illustrative.

In 1961 James Bryant Conant, former chemistry professor at Harvard and President of that institution from 1933 to 1953, received support from the Carnegie Corporation of New York to study teacher education. Two years and thousands of miles later, *The Education of American Teachers* was published.[3] It included a long list of specific recommendations for improving the quality of teachers. The context in which these recommendations were made should be noted. The United States was still reeling from the successes of the Soviet space program. American schools were bursting at the seams, trying to accommodate the offspring of the "baby boom." Public schools were desperate for teachers, a situation that gave rise to a variety of short-cuts to certification.

Enter James Bryant Conant. Zeroing in on what he perceived to be the counter-productive tension between professors of education and "academic" professors, he called for greater collaboration in the interests of quality schooling for American youth. He also urged more steadfast devotion to excellence, both in teacher training and in public education, and a sweeping reassessment of certification requirements.

Whether or not he intended it, Conant's observations and suggestions were regarded by many as a mandate for greater involvement by non-education professors in teacher education. The message to education faculty was clear. To be a respected member of the academic community, one must behave less like a teacher educator and more like an arts-and-sciences scholar. This meant conducting original research, writing for academic audiences rather than practitioners, and consulting with professors in the disciplines before developing new curricula for public schools.

Close on Conant's heels came James D. Koerner, one-time professor and staff member of the Council for Basic Education. In *The Miseducation of American Teachers*, Koerner displayed little of Conant's tact or genuine concern for collaboration.[4] His review of the literature on teacher education and visits to 63 accredited institutions where teachers were trained led him to conclude that teacher educators constitute "a sincere, humanitarian, well-intentioned, hard-working, poorly informed, badly educated, and ineffectual group of men and women."[5] A major cause for alarm to Koerner was the popular perception that Education faculty did not compare favorably with "academic" professors. Such a perception, he contended, compelled brighter college students to avoid careers in public education.

Once again, the message to teacher educators was clear. To establish respectability and attract more talented students, they would have to behave more like "academic" professors. More research must be done and less teaching and supervision. Teacher educators would have to work more closely with scholars in the disciplines. Presumably time for these new contacts would come at the expense of maintaining traditional ties to the field. The royal road to respectability apparently was one that did not often leave campus to venture into communities and public schools.

What is noteworthy about the work of Conant, Koerner, and others is the absence of any substantive set of recommendations concerning changes in the job of teaching. The suggestions—and there were dozens—focused almost exclusively on controlling input (the quality of teacher candidates, the quality of teacher educators, the college curriculum) and output (the high school curriculum, graduation requirements). The presumption was that cadres of talented new teachers trained by talented new academicians could produce a generation of bright new scientists by employing challenging new curriculum materials within the essentially unchanged context of the public school classroom. The naivete of these prescriptions only now is being appreciated.

For years after these recommendations were made, however, policymakers continued to focus on teacher preparation, teacher inservice, and public school standards and minimize the importance of altering how the work of the teacher was defined. The supply of new teachers, after all, was more than sufficient throughout the sixties and early seventies. With so little attention given to changes in the teacher's job, though, teacher educators had no alternative but continue to prepare teachers for conventional teaching positions. Policymakers, for their part, often feel that efforts to reconceptualize the job of teaching should come from higher education. They fail to realize that changes in the nature of teachers' work require changes in education policy, financial support, and school organization.

What did fifteen years of experimentation with teacher education produce? States have mandated competency-based teacher education programs and tests for teachers. Independent commissions have been established to oversee teacher certification programs. Pressure has come from "academic" professors to strengthen teacher preparation in the disciplines. Pressure has come from minority groups to train more minority educators and ensure that teachers can respond effectively to the needs of minority students. Pressure has come from educational R & D groups and commercial interests to adopt a variety of "packaged" programs guaranteed to help teachers deal with the disadvantaged, the gifted, the handicapped, the reluctant, and the unmotivated. The net impact of all these pressures, according to long-time schoolwatcher and philosopher Harry Broudy, has been to accelerate the "deprofessionalization of teacher education."[6] Like the teachers they supposedly train and serve, teacher educators are beset by too many panaceas, too few resources to implement them, and too little control over their own destinies.

After fifteen years of ferment and experimentation, B. Othanel Smith, in the lead article for *Phi Delta Kappan's* 1980 special issue on teacher education admitted,

> Let's face it: Colleges of pedagogy will in all probability never overhaul their programs if each college is to do it alone. There are too many hurdles, too much disparity among institutions, too much institutional jealousy, too much divisiveness and lethargy among faculties, too much fear, and too much ineptness in the leadership.[7]

Another article in the same special issue of *Phi Delta Kappan* analyzed the "professional component" of training programs for various professions, including teaching.[8] While training requirements for most professions have increased over the past half century, those for teaching have remained about the same. Considering the increase in demands and expectations for the performance of teachers over fifty years, this stability must be regarded with alarm. The article concludes with the observation that barbers in Florida, where the study was centered, are required to have 1500 hours of professional schooling before they can sit for examination, a total greater than the hours needed to become a secondary teacher!

Rather than an experience during which prospective teachers are provided with technical skills, endowed with professional attitudes, and inspired to settle for nothing less than the best they can achieve, preservice teacher training often is regarded as an obstacle to be overcome. Good teachers perceive they are effective in spite, rather than as a result, of teacher educators. Surveys of veteran teachers' inservice needs generally reveal a variety of skills and topics that were overlooked or treated too lightly during initial training—classroom management, diagnosing behavior disorders, dealing with handicapped students, coping with stress, resource allocation, education law, teacher rights, school organization, effective planning, and the list goes on and on. It seems that too much time during preservice training is spent on teaching methods and educational foundations and too little on familiarizing teachers with the realities of the professional world and helping them acquire the skills to feel efficacious. Thus, thousands of acolytes march off to classrooms each fall with the best of intentions, only to discover that the desire to help young people is but a place to begin, not to end.

What may be needed in preservice teacher education is more attention to "anticipatory socialization"—helping prospective teachers understand exactly what it will feel like to be a teacher. Writing of the need to reduce the likelihood that prospective teachers will be shocked when they start teaching, Sarason advocates a particular kind of pre-professional preparation:

> By "preparing" I do not mean "adjusting" them (teachers) to the realities. I mean giving them preparatory experiences, and a more realistic set of concepts than they now get, of what the school culture is (it is more than a classroom), of what it means to work with diverse people in diverse roles (a teacher is not only with children), and of how tensions between the individual and "the system" are inevitable (the needs of the individual and the system are by no means identical).[9]

Many Schools of Education are currently making concerted efforts to upgrade the quality of their preservice education. Among the strategies being employed are tightening admissions standards, strengthening curricula, offering more field-based experiences, and adding another year to the traditional four-year program.[10] Perhaps the most far-reaching change being discussed is the establishment of a set of tough new standards to guide the process by which education programs are nationally accredited.[11] Standards would cover faculty, financial and physical resources, admissions, governance, evaluation of graduates, and the "knowledge base." At present, however, failure by an education program to receive accreditation carries few negative consequences. Virtually no state or local school board *requires* its teachers to come from a program approved by the National Council for Accreditation of Teacher Education (NCATE).[12]

Inservice Education

Prospective teachers rarely know enough about their intended profession to lobby for changes in the preservice curriculum. Experienced teachers, on the other hand, are much clearer concerning what they need to know to function effectively on the job. Why, then, is there so much dissatisfaction with inservice education?[13] One obvious reason is that veteran teachers are not extensively involved in planning and implementing professional development activities.

In 1976 the National Education Association reported that about 68 percent of the teachers in a national survey participated in some form of inservice education—an increase of 10 percent since 1971.[14] The most common types of activities were workshops sponsored by central offices and college courses. These forms of inservice education, perhaps for economic reasons, tend to be highly generalized—aimed broadly at teachers from various subject matter areas, grade levels, and schools. Yarger, Howey, and Joyce found, in one study, that less than one teacher in five was involved in professional development activities specifically related to his or her work situation.[15]

While it is sometimes difficult for teachers to express their displeasure with district-sponsored workshops through non-participation, they are less reluctant to "vote with their feet" when it comes to college courses. When the NEA conducted another national survey in 1981, the percentage of teachers who had taken college courses during the year had dropped from 45 percent (1976) to 20 percent.[16]

The loss of inservice education revenues can seriously affect many college budgets. Like preservice education, inservice education is big business. Because official records on inservice education are notoriously poor, it is difficult to calculate how much money annually is spent to improve the skills of experienced teachers, but recent estimates range from 315 million to 2 billion dollars.[17] Given general economic conditions in the early eighties and the shrinkage in preservice programs, it is hardly surprising to find competition for inservice dollars has grown intense. Colleges, R & D centers, and private consultants trade inflated claims and deflating criticism. Inservice education has even been tainted by scandal, as 43 Los Angeles-area teachers were indicted in 1982 for accepting salary increases for extension courses they never attended.[18] The behavior of the teachers cannot be excused, but the college which permitted academic credit to be given under the circumstances must be condemned as well. The extent to which the Los Angeles case is indicative of conditions elsewhere is impossible to ascertain, but it is likely that other institutions of higher education have been guilty of comparable misrepresentation and fraud. Despite the alleged importance of inservice education, policies in this area are confused, if they exist at all. For example, consider the extensive criticism by teachers and school officials of the benefits of college-based professional development courses, as well as other types of inservice activities. Then realize that an increasing number of states are mandating that teachers, to keep their licenses current, *must* participate in inservice education. It hardly seems prudent to require teachers to take part in activities the value of which is yet to be demonstrated on any large-scale basis.

The basic issue is that colleges, universities, and most other purveyors of professional development services are primarily interested in their own survival and only secondarily concerned with providing the kind of assistance to teachers that teachers seek. These organizations are compelled for various reasons to work with existing personnel, even if some are not adept at inservice education or familiar with the realities of contemporary public schools. Milbrey McLaughlin and David Marsh, while persuaded that professors may never be able to enjoy the credibility of "insiders," speculate on several positive roles professors can play in the professional development process:

> . . . the ineffectiveness of outside consultants in the implementation process raises serious questions about the roles which universities can play in school-based staff development programs. It is clear that packaged inservice programs, especially those offered without extensive classroom follow-up and teacher participation, are not likely to be effective according to the Rand research. In turn, however, universities could play several creative roles. First, they could prepare administrators and other school leaders who are able to carry out the innovation process . . . Secondly, in their preservice teacher education programs, they could prepare teachers to play the secondary role of collaborative planner within a problem-solving dynamic organization.[19]

Despite the abundance of criticism directed at ineffectual inservice education, there are some hopeful signs, however. The knowledge base concerning what constitutes effective inservice education is rapidly expanding.[20] Teachers, often through their associations and unions, are playing more of a key role in decision making regarding professional development.[21] Finally, prestigious universities such as Yale and Syracuse have inaugurated collaborative professional development ventures with local school districts. David Imig, executive director of the American Association of Colleges for Teacher Education, adds that failure to pursue such collaborative efforts may say less about professional disinterest than the state of higher education budget systems.[22] As long as department budgets are based solely on the number of students attracted to campus, professors will face disincentives when working off-campus with groups of teachers.

Research and Development

Preservice and inservice education are not the only ways that colleges and universities may provide assistance to teachers. Scholars conduct research in learning, teacher and school effectiveness, and a variety of other topics as well as contributing to the development of new subject matter, curricula, instructional techniques, and school improvement programs. Some of these efforts have been truly beneficial. Studies of language acquisition, mathematical reasoning, and learning disabilities readily come to mind.[23] All too often, however, the influence of educational R & D has either been unproductive or a source of problems for practitioners. While I do not wish to imply that researchers have purposely set out to undermine the teaching profession, I believe that many of the problems caused by poor or insensitive research and development probably could have been minimized by greater cognizance of the world in which teachers work and the minimal resources typically available to them. The next chapter looks in greater detail at problems resulting from actual efforts to implement new ideas and techniques in schools. For now, the focus is more on the generation of knowledge.

It may be useful to begin with a brief overview of the R & D enterprise. Prior to the creation of the National Institute of Education in 1972, there was little basis at all for maintaining that any substantial portion of R & D efforts in the U.S. were part of a well-coordinated, comprehensive plan. The foci of research typically were dictated by the predilections of individual scholars, who, in turn, were often motivated to seek "unplowed turf" in the hopes of building their reputations and avoiding domain disputes with other academicians. The haphazard manner in which educational R & D was undertaken ensured that old ideas periodically would turn up with new labels.

Despite the problems with early efforts, it at least can be said that scholars tended to investigate issues which mattered to educators. This era predated the writings of Conant and Koerner and the time when faculties of professional schools would be judged according to the same criteria as faculties of academic departments. Professors of education typically came up through the ranks, serving first as classroom teachers and school administrators. Since large government and private foundation grants for R & D still lay in the future, professors could not afford to ignore the concerns of educators, even when they were disposed to do so. Their institutions' survival depended on the tuitions paid by teachers-in-training and experienced teachers seeking advanced degrees.

The forties and fifties were characterized, in fact, by the "action research" movement—an effort to stimulate research in schools and classrooms through the collaborative efforts of teachers, administrators, and professors. What determined the nature of "action research"—unlike much of the "programatic research" and conceptual work which has characterized more recent times—was the likelihood of solving a particular, localized concern. The desire for "generalizability"—research results which could be applied with equal validity to large numbers of schools, students, or teachers—was not the obsession it has now become.

With the sixties came pressure for education professors to be more like their colleagues in the sciences. Funds from government agencies and private foundations became available to help them undertake the transformation. No longer were many scholars solely dependent on their academic salaries for a livelihood. In turn, colleges and universities did not have to rely as much on tuitions for economic survival. The National Science Foundation poured millions of dollars into curriculum development work in the basic sciences, mathematics, and certain social sciences. This work brought education professors into direct contact with "academic" professors and produced "The New Math," "The New Biology," "The New Physics," and so on. Their collaboration generated shelves of new texts, workbooks, and other learning materials, but little in the way of demonstrated improvements in student achievement or teaching.

In his studies of the failure of many school improvement efforts, Seymour Sarason tersely characterizes the curriculum reform movements of the sixties as merely a substitution of one set of books for another.[24] He attributes much of the problem to naivete on the part of professors—lack of awareness that curriculum change also requires changes in the "culture of the school." As an illustration, he observes that those responsibile for the "New Math" underestimated what would be needed to equip teachers with the skills necessary to implement new curricula. Goals were always stated in terms of student outcomes, rather than teacher outcomes. The implication of such simplistic thinking was that teachers trained for years in one type of mathematics could acquire during a summer workshop or two sufficient understanding of a different approach to mathematics to become competent New Math instructors. When the teachers failed in many cases to acquire such understanding, the professors blamed them for lack of intelligence rather than seeing the problem as a result of poor planning and unrealistic expectations.

Despite the disappointments of the curriculum reform efforts, education faculty continued to look to "academic" faculty for leadership. Schools of Education began to hire more individuals who were trained in the disciplines. Once regarded as service areas, fields such as sociology of education, educational anthropology, and economics of education grew to positions of influence rivalling those of curriculum and instruction. From the sixties on, it was not uncommon in the more prestigious Schools of Education to find professors who had never been employed in the public schools. A leading teacher effectiveness researcher, N.L. Gage, signaled this trend when he wrote,

We have not been getting an adequate supply of educational research workers. . . . The school of education that first invents an arrangement for enticing bright young persons directly from their undergraduate work into graduate school for training as educational research workers will become for educational research what Johns Hopkins was for medical research. . . .[25]

With experience in public education devalued by professors and with more non-educators moving into educational research, it was predictable that the gulf between the world of the teacher and the world of the professor would widen. Just how this gap has developed can be seen in the following examples.

Lack of commitment. As many education faculty were prompted to take more of their cues from "academic" faculty, they increasingly were perceived by teachers as insensitive to the day-to-day problems associated with instructing students. This fact has even been acknowledged to be a problem by a President of the American Educational Research Association (AERA). Addressing the 1982 meeting AERA, William Cooley maintained:

> We have miles to go to establish dialogue with practitioners. We need to put together research in a way that is interpretable to those in the schools.[26]

New faculty members in the most influential Schools of Education have earned little credit toward tenure for selecting problems on which to work that are meaningful to teachers. Those who do survive have learned, instead, to choose problems that are judged conceptually or theoretically important by senior professors. Since senior professors are not likely to have spent much time in recent years in schools, the problems they value often have little relationship to the concerns of teachers. It is not uncommon for a young education professor, when confronted by a problem of consequence to teachers, to ask: "Does this problem have the potential to yield a publication or enhance my reputation among my senior colleagues?" rather than "How can I draw upon the existing body of research and theory to help these practitioners?" In order to answer the former question, the young professor must consider such matters as the novelty of the problem (new problems are more apt to be interesting than old problems) and the scope of the problem (problems with too much complexity are too difficult for researchers to control). As a result, the problems that often receive attention from researchers are not the ones which teachers would tend to select. Of this process, Roald Campbell, a senior educational researcher, writes:

> Many recent appointments in schools of education . . . have been filled with persons prepared in social psychology,

sociology, political science, and in other disciplines. Those appointments have been made with the conviction that such persons would bring new insights and help transform the field. . . . But, in many instances, representatives of the disciplines have simply used the schools as a convenient arena in which to continue investigations pertinent to their respective disciplines. In short, educational phenomena have served the disciplines instead of the disciplines being brought to bear upon educational problems.[27]

Technism. Kenneth Keniston describes *technism* as a prevailing contemporary ideology that "places central value on what can be measured with numbers, assigns numbers to what cannot be measured, and redefines everything else as self-expression or entertainment."[28] Technism has contributed to the undervaluing of problems that matter to teachers, since they typically do not easily lend themselves to quantification. Such "messy" problems often involve relationships between people, time and resource management, professional growth, and student attitudes. Many researchers feel more comfortable working with averages on standardized achievement tests, test-item analyses, comparative statistics on dropout or attendance, and similar "low-inference" or "hard" data.

Not only does technism lead researchers to overlook issues that matter to teachers, but it fosters research that drastically over-simplifies the world in which teachers work. These studies undermine morale, create confusion, and often persuade policymakers to allocate resources in ways that make the job of teaching even more difficult. The work of James Coleman and his associates is illustrative. A sociologist by training, Coleman has conducted several major studies of relevance to education. His work in the sixties comparing student achievement across different types of public schools concluded, among other things, that the quality of teachers and their instruction accounted for little of the between-school variance in student achievement.[29] Despite criticisms of his methodology, sampling techniques, and achievement measures, Coleman's work was interpreted by many policymakers to mean that investing funds in teacher training and development was unwise economically.

In 1981 Coleman published another largescale study, this one comparing student achievement in public and nonpublic schools.[30] Once again, the study was criticized for a variety of methodological problems.[31] Once again, policymakers took careful note of the results. And, once again, the impact on public school teachers promised to be harmful. Coleman's findings supposedly demonstrated that teachers in public schools are less successful than private school teachers.

Fear exists that the publicity given the study will cause public schools to lose even more of their capable students. Similarly, the aftermath of Coleman's earlier work had been "white flight" from urban to suburban schools. The spectre of growing concentrations of lower ability students in urban public schools already faced with economic problems is a source of serious concern to teachers.

Additional indications of the insensitivity of researchers to teachers can be found in the way they express their conclusions. For instance, a comprehensive review of research on performance-based teacher education in an influential journal concluded that:

> given the well-documented, strong association between student achievement and variables such as socioeconomic status and ethnic status, the effects of techniques of teaching on achievement . . . are likely to be inherently trivial.[32]

And the following statement from a leading textbook on sociology of education:

> There is little empirical support for the assumption that a "happy worker is a better worker," which seems to be a major principle behind attempts to increase the job satisfaction of workers.[33]

What is one to make of these "scientific" statements? Only that they are statements by scientists. Is it possible that the happiness of teachers makes no difference because a significant statistical relationship between productivity and happiness is elusive? Should schools be staffed with high school dropouts because teaching skill cannot be shown statistically to be an important factor in student achievement? Most researchers, of course, would disavow such exaggerations. Yet, they often fail to realize the potential for misinterpretation carried by their statements.

Illusion of awareness. Coleman's work gave rise to certain negative inferences about teachers, but it did not directly involve studies of teachers. There have been, however, thousands of studies that attempted to hone in on exactly what teachers do in class. Many of these studies conducted over the last two decades have been grouped under the rubric of "teacher effectiveness" or "process-product" research. The typical teacher effectiveness study identifies some teacher behavior (process variable) and attempts to correlate it with some measure of student achievement (product). Frequently preliminary observations are made of exemplary teachers in order to determine which teacher behaviors merit analysis.

While early teacher effectiveness studies generally failed to yield many significant relationships between teacher behavior and student achievement, more recent research has begun to find that certain factors—such as teacher expectations and time devoted to direct instruction—may be associated with student success.[34]

The problem with teacher effectiveness research is not the finding that what teachers do in classrooms makes a difference, but the implication that, if teachers are only made aware of what they are not doing that they should be doing (or vice versa), they will have the resources and organizational support necessary to change. The "illusion" that awareness alone is a sufficiently useful outcome of research activity has kept teachers and researchers at arm's length for years. Teachers contend that they have long known, even without sophisticated studies, what must be done to produce greater student achievement. What typically is lacking is the time, security, support personnel, materials, parental support, and building leadership needed to implement more effective teaching strategies. The present ethos of austerity only promises to exacerbate the problem.

An analogy may be useful. Consider the case of a homely person who, for lack of a mirror, is unaware that he is quite as unattractive as he really is. He knows he could be better looking to be sure, but this vague sense does not prevent him from living a relatively productive life. A helpful cosmetologist comes along with a mirror and demonstrates to the homely person how truly ugly he is. A detailed comparison is made between the homely person's features and those of movie stars. Then, the cosmetologist departs.

The homely person is crestfallen. He realizes that he lacks the money necessary for plastic surgery or other cosmetological treatments. At the same time, he is unable to return to his relatively productive, pre-mirror days, since his vague notions of being unattractive have now been confirmed by an outside expert. His confidence plummets and he avoids contact with other people. He grows resentful that he cannot afford to correct his ugliness, while others have more money than they need.

The question is—Has the cosmetologist done the homely person a favor?

PROFESSORS V. PEDAGOGUES

What should be a natural alliance among professionals concerned about the quality of schooling in the U.S. threatens at times to become an open rivalry. There are many reasons for the growing adversarial relations besides those just discussed. Professors increasingly express themselves in a technical argot that serves more to keep practitioners at a distance than encourage understanding. Schools of Education, motivated perhaps by self-interest, press for more requirements for prospective teachers and mandatory inservice training for experienced teachers, thus expanding the commitments of time and money needed to be a teacher. Many teachers feel that teacher educators have precious little to offer them already without increasing requirements. The research done by professors, many of whom lack intimate or recent knowledge of public schools, often is employed by critics of teachers to attack public education.

As if there were not sufficient reasons for antagonism between teachers and professors, the present era of retrenchment could intensify ill will. Teachers and professors are forced to compete for diminishing resources from federal, state and local governments. Even within higher education, the signs of strained relations are evident. Teacher educators complain that researchers do not pull their teaching load, while researchers counter that teacher educators lack the scholarly productivity to attract research grants. In the process of battling for a piece of the shrinking fiscal pie, the goals of education can easily slip from view.

In theory, however, retrenchment could cause teachers and professors to draw closer together. Higher education, for example, must rely to an increasing extent on tuition monies as research grants and government support dwindles. As public school budgets are cut, teachers have a greater need for research that will help them maintain quality services with fewer resources. Perhaps, if the economy continues its downturn, this "natural alliance" between concerned educators can finally be forged. Policymakers will need to be sensitive to this possibility if it is to be more than a fantasy.

CHAPTER 7

School Improvement Efforts and the Negative Side of Noble Ambitions

This book is essentially an analysis of the unrealized expectations and disappointments of the contemporary public school teacher. Perhaps in no other area of schooling is the likelihood of unrealized expectations and disappointments greater than school improvement efforts. It is a domain in which well-intentioned policymakers and hard-working teachers frequently appear to travel parallel, but rarely intersecting paths.

The "change process"—as it has been dubbed by scholars studying school improvement efforts—sometimes finds teachers unable to look beyond their particular job situations and comprehend the larger context in which change needs to occur. Policymakers, on the other hand, may overlook the fact that individuals have a limited capacity for change—even presumably positive change.

Dan Lortie has maintained, "People attracted to teaching tend to favor the status quo."[1] He attributes this proclivity to characteristics of the processes by which teachers are trained and recruited. What Lortie fails to note is the fact that the job of teaching itself may cause teachers to shrink from innovations. It is not that teachers by nature and selection are resistant to change. Rather, so much change is built into the teacher's world in the form of new students each year, faculty and administrative turnover, new mandates, and curriculum modifications that teachers may not appreciate school improvement projects—however promising.

At no time in American history have there existed more groups dedicated to the process of improving schools. State Departments of Education and their regional units. The federal Department of Education and a host of other agencies with at least a minor interest in elementary and secondary education. Private foundations. Interest groups, ranging from school boards associations and organizations of school administrators to the John Birch Society and the Children's Defense League. The variety is impressive. Besides a general concern with the quality of schooling, the only characteristic these agencies and interest groups seem to share is a perception that other bodies wield more influence. It is a curious fact that virtually every group with a stake in the schools feels it either has lost power in recent years or never had power. State government feels it has lost authority to the federal bureaucracy. Local districts complain that state and intermediate agencies have usurped many of their prerogatives. School administrators complain that collective bargaining has resulted in the loss of considerable control. Teachers point out that the growth of school advisory groups and citizens' lobbies has made them more vulnerable to political pressure.

Whether or not all these groups could lose power simultaneously is not the issue. If people *perceive* they lack sufficient influence, they band together to form interest groups, pay lobbyists, and put pressure on government agencies and elected representatives. The result has been the increasing politicization of public schooling.

By virtue of their key role in the educational enterprise, teachers often find themselves the focus of political activity. This activity can be crudely divided into two basic types. One type aims to improve schooling by chastising, regulating, or circumventing teachers. The other type of activity focuses on helping teachers tackle jobs that seem to grow more complex annually. It is easy to understand how the former efforts serve to demoralize teachers and drive them from the profession. Ironically, however, many attempts to help teachers turn out to do more harm than good. Noble ambitions, it would appear, are no guarantee that innovations will leave schools and teachers better off than they were before. This chapter describes how teachers may be victimized or discouraged by the efforts of planners and policymakers to improve the quality of public schools.

THE NEGATIVE BY-PRODUCTS OF CHANGE

Until recently the major mechanisms for school improvement were external funding and outside expertise. Federal and state governments and private foundations spawned an assortment of schemes, including Title I and Title IV-C projects, Teacher Corps, Experimental Schools program, California's School Improvement Plan, the Kettering Foundation's Individually Guided Education, and the Ford Foundation's decentralization plans for New York City. Each of these programs involved local schools in the complex process of systematic improvement, a rational process which supposedly begins with planning, moves to implementation, and concludes with careful evaluation of progress. As the following analysis suggests, the potential at each of these stages for "negative by-products" for teachers has been considerable.

The Planning Stage

When policymakers launch school improvement efforts, their motives for the most part are unselfish and beyond reproach. It would be naive, however, to pretend that all changes were free of less noble desires—career advancement, institutional visibility, monetary gain, and so on. When teachers sense these motives, they become disenchanted and resentful. For now, however, I wish to consider *how* proposals for change are planned rather than *why*. In all but the luckiest circumstances, school improvement efforts can be no better than the quality of the initial plans.

What aspects of planning school improvement tend to foster job-related problems for teachers?

One troublesome characteristic of most planning efforts is the sense of urgency. Requests for proposals typically require considerable time for brainstorming, assessing needs, collaborative goal setting, securing the consent of proposed participants, devising a budget, and preparing the finished proposal. These tasks all must be completed by a specific deadline. Working under severe time constraints, as is often the case, is hardly conducive to good morale or planning. Anneke and Eric Bredo observe that when time limitations interfere, the planning stage of an innovation can produce a host of vague "symbolic agreements."[2] Once the plans are put into operation, the "unsolved technical difficulties" and "unresolved goal conflicts" that have been set aside in order to complete the proposal return to haunt the project.

Collaborative planning among educators and community representatives has been a requirement of some proposals for school improvement. While in theory involving different interest groups seems a desirable, democratic thing to do, realistically it often is impossible. Innovators sometimes resort to creating an impression that decision making has been collaborative, while failing in actuality to make certain that the people who will be affected by the innovation approve of it. Little time is spent anticipating potentially negative by-products of change or building strong personal allegiances to a project. As a result of such oversights, at least one teacher, commenting on unsuccessful innovations in New York City, has concluded that

> all efforts to institutionalize large-scale change in New York City schools are doomed to failure because the line teacher has no input into the reform effort.[3]

A third factor that can contribute to planning problems is the tendency of those seeking to make an impact to overcommit themselves. In the spirit of political campaign promises, innovators produce long lists of objectives in order to increase the probability of gaining a funding agency's support. Funding agencies do little to discourage overcommitment. Sometimes the authors of funding proposals sincerely believe that educational change can result only from multiple objectives. This belief in comprehensive change is typified by one description of the ambitious Model Schools Project (supported by the National Association of Secondary School Principals) as an "outgrowth of our conviction and experiences that only 'total commitment to total change' will produce significantly improved schools."[4] In a similar vein, the Teacher Corps required applicants for grants to address a variety of "add-ons" (the Teachers Corps' own mandated objectives, ranging from multicultural education to competency based teacher education) in addition to the applicants' original objectives. One study of the Teacher Corps concludes that major problems developed because the particular projects under investigation attempted "to achieve multiple goals that were in partial conflict with one another."[5]

Writing about problems experienced by school systems that participated in the federally funded Experimental Schools (ES) program, Michael Kirst observes,

> The ES program is a classic case of multiple, vague, and somewhat contradictory federal objectives that leave LEAs (Local Educational Authorities) confused about federal desires. . . . "Comprehensive change" is more a slogan than a concept to guide operations. Consequently, the LEAs could include everything and anything and were never required to be very precise. Arcadia's goals were "humanizing and individualizing," Shiloh County wanted to "individualize diagnostic instruction," and Jackson County aspired to a "coordinated program . . . for . . . improving the quality and relevance of education for all pupils." In view of the ES desire for comprehensive change, there was apparently little federal assistance in scaling down overly ambitious local projects to meet local capabilities.[6]

Who suffers when school improvement plans are allowed to be "overly ambitious"? Those who must carry out the plans—teachers—typically bear the burden of unrealistic goals. The burden is less onerous when teachers play an active role in the planning process, but extensive teacher participation has been more the exception than the rule in school improvement efforts.[7]

It can be argued that time constraints, illusory collaborative plan-ning, and the tendency to pursue too many objectives simultaneously are structural problems—in other words, that they are built into the very process by which innovations are externally funded. There are other planning problems, however, that derive from the planners and policymakers themselves.

Harry Wolcott has identified three characteristics that distinguish how teachers think about change from the ways planners and pol-icymakers—or "technocrats" to use Wolcott's term—think about change.[8] The differences involve time orientation, orientation toward authority, and personal style. Technocrats tend to cultivate impa-tience, value hierarchy, and concentrate resources on specific objec-tives, according to Wolcott. Teachers, on the other hand, may require time to adjust to the idea of change, discretionary authority to modify innovations to fit their own particular situations, and somewhat flexible objectives.

Teachers' readiness for change is a critical factor in determining the ultimate success of school improvement.[9] Unfortunately, teachers are not always questioned in a systematic manner to discover their level of readiness. Willingness does not equal readiness. A given school may become involved in a change project simply because (1) it is close to a sponsoring university, (2) the superintendent or building principal desires a project, or (3) outside funds become available. None of these reasons alone is sufficient to justify the school's involvement in large-scale change. Certain questions must first be asked.

Is the faculty prepared for large-scale change? Are they able and willing to devote the time necessary to plan and acquire new skills? Do they share the perception that change is necessary? Even if teachers agree that change is justified, they may still resist an in-novation if they feel that too many external demands have been placed on them over too brief a time period. Preceding chapters suggest that the environments in which most teachers work have grown so unstable and become subject to so many different com-munity and government expectations that even worthy change efforts sometimes are perceived as problems.

I have briefly described one kind of change process myopia—the type that blinds planners and policymakers to the organizational and individual realities with which they must deal. A second type prevents these individuals from foreseeing the full effects of the changes they are proposing.[10] In particular, they often fail to realize that change often involves redefining roles. William Smith, past Director of the Teacher Corps, made no secret of the fact that improving education required role changes: "All with a role or an investment in the education of kids must be involved in the change process, in roles of equality to whatever extent possible."[11] Despite Smith's open declaration, many Teacher Corps projects failed to provide for the gradual acquisition of new roles by teachers, to create extrinsic rewards for those expected to change, or to guide administrators whose roles also were subject to change. The Teacher Corps and its projects ultimately were judged by the changes they brought about in students. Perhaps for this reason, changes in teachers and administrators did not receive adequate attention.

Arthur Stinchcombe has warned that serious problems can result when planners overlook the side effects of requiring people (1) to learn new roles; (2) to change roles, which involves "high costs in time, worry, conflict, and temporary inefficiency; (3) to work with strangers, which requires the development of some degree of trust; and (4) to redirect established loyalties.[12] Many innovations stall or fail when teachers become uneasy because of unanticipated pressures such as these. The presence of new faces at school, for example, cannot help but raise the level of suspicion. A study of early Teacher Corps projects finds that the policy of using freshly trained interns full of new ideas to "cause teachers and principals to adopt new positions" failed to produce desired changes.[13] In fact, the greater the differences between the views of the interns and those of school personnel, the fewer changes were found to occur.

Sometimes problems derive less from a change agent's alien status in the school or his briefcase full of new ideas than from the failure to give sufficient attention to re-educating teachers. As indicated earlier, Sarason has observed that the absence of positive results at a given school that had adopted the New Math occurred in part because the project's objectives were written in terms of changes in students rather than changes in teachers.[14] Of course, teachers have to learn the New Math themselves and feel comfortable with it before their students can be expected to benefit, but this essential step had been omitted—a costly oversight.

The Implementation Stage

The implementation stage of school improvement may be defined, in a somewhat circular manner, as that stage for which the planning stage was impatiently endured.

Unfortunately, the dreams of planners and policymakers often turn into nightmares during implementation.[15] Teachers begin to complain that they are expected to do too much. Faculty morale plummets. Administrators find practitioners uncooperative and critical. To avoid embarrassment, they place increased pressure on teachers to produce results. Negative attitudes and disillusionment increase. Why?

The reasons are complex. A basic assumption underlying most changed efforts, for example, is that something is not right with the existing situation. Contributing to a review of the federal government's role in educational reform, Mario Fantini observed that innovations sometimes "base their own existence on the shortcomings of conventional programs, that is, in order to justify the innovation, criticism is levelled at what is."[16] Thus a school improvement proposal may reflect adversely on the very people expected to implement it— teachers. It thus can be argued that teachers often have a vested interest in seeing that innovations fail. Failure is vindication, a statement that maybe teachers have been performing better than planners and policymakers thought.

Imagine a typical project from a teacher's point of view. The reason for the project is apparent: the students are not doing as well as they should. Perhaps not as clearly stated by change agents, but certainly implied, is the assumption that the teachers have not been completely successful diagnosing student needs and providing appropriate instruction. Outside resource people begin to arrive at the school. They lack credibility in the teachers' eyes ("What do they know about *our* school?"). Meetings are scheduled (remember that there already have been innumerable meetings during the planning stage). Soon the teachers feel that the project, rather than making their jobs more manageable (usually a reasonable expectation with any school improvement project), actually requires more time and work than before.

One of the curious and inexplicable verities of change efforts is that they rarely seem to reach the point where the required meetings actually diminish. In an evaluation of the Alum Rock, California, voucher project, for instance, note was taken of the costs to teachers in terms of time and energy:

> Almost all of the voucher teachers reported working extra hours. Fifty percent, in fact, reported working six or more extra hours per week compared to the previous year. Some of the extra demands on teachers' time seemed especially burdensome: 88 percent cited "too many meetings" as a main disadvantage of the demonstration, and 69 percent cited "too much paperwork."[17]

Project administrators view meetings as opportunities to solve problems, but teachers frequently regard meetings as work—and relatively unproductive work at that. Since problems seem to multiply as projects age, the number of meetings continues to grow until teachers begin to complain that they no longer have time to plan their lessons or teach. In *Schoolteacher,* Dan Lortie provides strong evidence of how much teachers resent time demands that do not yield direct benefits for classroom instruction.[18] Not only are meetings perceived to intrude on teachers' instructional time and private time, but they can reduce the time available for productive faculty interaction.

Several months into a project teachers may begin to question where the payoff is. Perhaps prematurely, they cast about for benefits to students and themselves. Failing to notice positive changes in *their* students or themselves, teachers begin to lose the energy with which they initially approached project objectives. At this point project managers are faced with one of the fundamental conflicts of the school improvement process. What teachers generally perceive as help is not what outside planners and policymakers may perceive as help. This "perceptual dissonance" finds outsiders interpreting help in terms of making teachers more "aware" of their problems and their students' problems. Teachers, on the other hand, insist they know their problems already. Being made aware of existing problems without being presented with the tools for alleviating them is regarded as more a curse than a blessing. Teachers want specific solutions to problems and demonstrations of how the solutions work. As noted in the last chapter, change agents often are ill equipped to satisfy either of these desires.

The combination of extra work and little discernible improvement can damage faculty morale. An excellent account of this process in an innovating junior high school is presented by the Bredos. They conclude that trying to improve the school became "an extremely upsetting experience" for teachers.[19] Role confusion, unequal project responsibilities, and too many meetings all compounded the problem. Forrest Parkay offers further evidence of the backfire effects of change. He describes how faculty morale dropped in a Chicago high school when an outside consulting group contracted to assist in implementing year-round education. Parkay writes that the teachers were offended because the consultants ignored their battle-wise insights into the problems of their inner-city school.[20]

It is unfortunate when teachers are obliged to participate in a school improvement project that reinforces the notion that they do not know what they are doing. The result is often a cynical attitude toward improvement in general. Another undesirable by-product may be increased interpersonal tensions. For example, some teachers may find themselves working harder on a project than others. These individuals begin to feel either superior to their colleagues or taken advantage of. Other teachers may react with feelings of neglect when a project fails to focus on their areas of interest or concern. Teachers of elective courses, for instance, may feel that the basic skills curriculum gets all the attention. They may develop a sense of unimportance and begin to act as peripheral members of the school community. Resentments generated during some projects do not dissipate until long after the projects have terminated.

Would these bad feelings have surfaced if attention had been devoted to building trust in the initial stage of the project? There is some evidence to indicate that early attention to developing a climate for change pays off in terms of faculty cooperation. Climates for change, however, do not automatically emerge from a preliminary workshop or faculty retreat. Louis Smith and Pat Keith describe how even an intensive summer workshop prior to the opening of a new open-space elementary school failed to ensure harmonious relations among teachers and administrators or generate a clear notion of what was expected of participants. In fact, there was some evidence that the month-long workshop actually created problems of its own.![21] The naive faith that exposing project participants to a few group dynamics techniques will create trust and project allegiance among individuals accustomed to working in isolation borders on belief in magic. Care must be taken to cultivate positive attitudes toward the project and toward change *before* implementation begins. Unfortunately, it takes time to nurture attitudes, and time is usually scarce in any school improvement project.

I have reviewed some of the more obvious ways in which efforts to innovate may contribute to low teacher morale and stress. School improvement projects can also backfire in more subtle ways.

The imperative of the new idea. Very few projects are funded because they promise to implement a well-established program or replicate a practice of proven worth. Money flows to those who propose unique solutions to problems. New ideas—or old ideas carefully disguised to appear new—capture the imagination of funding agencies. There are few extrinsic rewards for educators who wish to work with the "best existing practices" or to modify credible, time-tested programs. In exclusively valuing that which appears to be new, those who seek to encourage the improvement of education actually devalue the successes of the past—many of which have been products of teacher initiative.

Goal displacement. No matter how admirable a project's initial goals may be, they can be displaced as a result of the exigencies of the funding game. The project's survival can replace school improvement as the primary goal.[22] Individuals who directly benefit from the project—those who derive salaries, prestige, or research data from it—sometimes conceal information about the project that might jeopardize refunding. Goal displacement leads project managers to overlook or minimize signs of tension and discontent among project participants.

Protecting one's own interests is understandable within certain limits. Unfortunately, these limits can be overstepped when goal displacement leads to self-delusion or unethical conduct on the part of those with a personal stake in a project's survival. For example, project managers may convince themselves that, despite the elusiveness of "hard data," their project is making a favorable impact. A wealth of factors are "discovered" to explain the lack of expected results: "We didn't have enough time or money. The community was resistant. The teachers were uncooperative." Such excuse-making can seriously undermine staff morale.

The Evaluation Stage

Utilizing external funds in an attempt to improve the quality of public schooling usually requires an evaluation of the project. Evaluation is the primary process by which funders expect to determine whether or not their money has been well spent. Formal evaluations, however, are not foolproof or uniformly beneficial. Evaluations can even leave schools with worse problems than they were encountering before the evaluations were conducted.

The most obvious example of an evaluation backfire effect occurs when evaluation is unsystematic, inappropriate, or poorly conducted. A specific illustration of improper evaluation concerns the New Math curriculum materials. Edward Begle, one of the developers of the New Math, noted that student achievement in New Math programs typically was assessed using tests originally designed to measure achievement in traditional mathematics programs.[23] Such a practice is akin to determining the winner of a boxing match by comparing the number of punches thrown by each fighter. The current controversy over group intelligence and achievement tests dramatizes the growing concerns over the serious consequences of evaluation techniques that as yet are far from infallible.

Even if the evaluation design is sound, the problem of premature evaluation can still arise. A report submitted to the President by the National Advisory Council on Education Professions Development identified the following weaknesses, among others, in policies and practices associated with project evaluation:[24]

1. Premature evaluation of a project or venture, made before it is fully operational.

2. Preoccupation with so-called "hard data" developed by mass use of standardized tests.
3. Too much concern with final results alone, leading to lack of effort to determine why project objectives were or were not met.

The negative by-products of premature evaluation, particularly where evaluators are obsessed with "hard data" and "final results," manifest themselves in faculty suspicions and unwillingness to co-operate. If time has not been set aside to cultivate a proper attitude toward evaluation, there is great risk that evaluation efforts will be subverted by teachers who feel threatened by the possibility of either being judged inadequate by outsiders or losing face among colleagues. Furthermore, given the general ethos of uncertainty characterizing the job of teaching, it would not be surprising to find some teachers who were unsure about whether or not project evaluation data might be used against them in the regular teacher evaluation process. Despite the legitimate need for project assessment data, it should be recognized that collecting information too early can lead to teacher paranoia and adversarial relationships between evaluators and teachers. Egon Guba underscores this point when he acknowledges that evaluation actually may be "dysfunctional to human performance."[25] Is arbitrary or premature evaluation worth the possible failure of the project being evaluated? Some evaluators, unfortunately, seem prepared to respond in the affirmative.

A third disadvantage that can result from project evaluation is the possibility that the evaluation design will determine the objectives of the project. Evaluation designs can lead planners to disregard any objectives that cannot be measured easily. As a result, legitimate project goals such as improved school climate and teacher-student relationships may be displaced by increased scores on standardized tests. In his foreward to Ronald Corwin's book on the Teacher Corps, Melvin Tumin contends that no sound evaluation of programs such as Title I and Head Start is possible without severely restricting the process of adapting new ideas to localized contexts.[26] In her analysis of the evaluation of California's Early Childhood Education program, Carolyn Denham concurs with Tumin:

> Unless evaluation is to be a tail wagging the dog, evaluators as well as legislators may have to accept the idea that some desirable program designs are not subject to evaluation of overall program effects. Indeed, centralized product evaluation is fundamentally antithetical to local control. It is counterproductive because it introduces pressures for

centralization that undermine the advantages of creative-local control.[29]

Whether it means living under the Sword of Damocles of external evaluation or dealing with the enervating process of planning and implementing new programs, school improvement has the potential to discourage teachers. Government officials, foundation representatives, private consultants, and project managers are often too quick to condemn teachers for resistance to change. The foregoing analysis suggests that teachers may have good reason to regard change efforts cautiously. The fact is that outside change agents may be the only consistent beneficiaries of innovation.[28] Ernest House, in a study of large scale educational innovation, concludes:

> Those who must most forcefully bear the burden of . . . innovation receive the fewest tangible rewards from the process, while those higher in the vertical division of labor benefit most.[29]

FROM TOO MUCH HELP TO TOO LITTLE

Though the sixties and seventies can be characterized as an era during which school improvement was encouraged without always providing for adequate involvement of teachers or anticipating possible backfire effects, at least the spirit of the times was largely constructive and pro-public education. The eighties seem to have ushered in a strikingly different era. The policies of the Reagan administration call for dismantling much of the federal educational bureaucracy, reducing funding for special programs such as Chapter I, and eliminating many of the regulations intended to promote equal educational opportunity. At the same time, attempts are being made to provide great assistance for private and parochial schools. Critics of tax credit and voucher schemes argue that these plans will result in further fragmentation of American society, with middle class students and the most talented students from poorer homes moving out of public schools. The spectre of a public school system serving only the poor, the non-white, and the low-achieving youngster may be sufficiently disturbing to dissuade some prospective teachers from entering the profession.

The diminishing federal role in education is counterbalanced by increased state intervention and pressure from local parent groups and lobbies. State legislatures have enacted or proposed a variety of measures to ensure accountability and improve performance in the schools. For example, proficiency tests for graduation have been mandated. Competency tests for teachers are being required in some states. In other words, deregulation, shifts in the loci of decision making, and alterations in educational funding have not meant that teachers are subject to less change. The changes are just of a different nature.

In addition, the increase in state requirements and regulations thus far has not been acccompanied by substantial amounts of additional resources to local schools. As a result, educators feel that they are expected to accomplish more with less. The mounting pressure of parent groups has contributed an element of hostility and defensiveness to the climate of retrenchment. Consensus among these groups on how the schools should be improved is non-existent. Teachers perceive they are caught in a crossfire of conflicting expectations. Their professional judgments regarding the academic needs of young people are drowned out by the cries of those who want the schools to advance parochial interests. From the Moral Majority's strident calls for book censorship, school prayer, and the teaching of creationism to the efforts of parents of handicapped students to gain greater individualization of instruction and sensitivity to their children's special needs, teachers today are confronted by a withering array of demands—some justified, some not. Almost any contemporary educational activity—be it a school closure, a new textbook, or bargaining for a contract—is sure to foment some disturbance or negative reaction.

To protect themselves, teachers have been compelled to become more "political." Unable to rely on traditional sources of support in the face of mounting public pressure, teachers devote increasing energy to union and association activities, grievance procedures, monitoring board meetings and legislative proceedings, and fundraising for the campaigns of supportive public officials. While they recognize that such efforts are needed for professional survival, some teachers privately admit that they did not enter the teaching profession to become politicians. They also realize that their increasing political activity, in turn, provokes greater community distrust and resentment. Once again, teachers' original expectations seem to clash with the reality of teaching today. The next chapter explores some of the ways in which teachers have tried to help themselves.

CHAPTER 8

Teachers Helping Teachers—
Does the Patient Have the Cure?

The trend in some contemporary medical circles is to encourage patients to take greater responsibility for curing themselves. At times, this movement comes close to an exercise in "blaming the victim," as the sick and distressed are indicted for poor diets, failure to exercise, and wanton neglect of bodily danger signals. In other cases, health workers seem content to point out that the sick typically are in a much better position to assist in their own recovery than outsiders.

In a similar vein, today's teachers could be enjoined to take more of a leadership role in helping themselves and their beleaguered profession. Theoretically, there are a number of possible forms which self-assistance could take. Collegial evaluation and peer-organized professional development are but two ideas. Between theory and reality, however, sit a series of obstacles, not the least of which are the school's organizational structure and, on occasion, teachers themselves. In this chapter, I wish to look at some ways in which teachers potentially might contribute to making their jobs more attractive and fulfilling and then describe several inhibitors to self-help. The chapter closes with a brief discussion of teacher unionization and collective bargaining and an assessment of current threats to negotiated gains made over the past several decades.

POTENTIAL FOR SELF-HELP

The "conventional wisdom" of schooling—wisdom frequently supported by empirical research—holds that teachers learn best from other teachers.[1] As indicated in Chapter 6, college professors often are too removed from the daily routines and problems of classrooms to be perceived as pertinent or credible. Educational literature is loaded with social science jargon that sacrifices utility for conceptual specificity. Administrators are not always judged to be experts on instructional matters. In addition, they may be regarded as too threatening to confide in, since they are responsible for teacher evaluation. Teachers, if they seek help at all, are therefore likely to turn to colleagues.

Lortie has found, however, that the matter of teachers helping teachers is far from simple.[2] Teachers are characterized by their individualism, a trait traceable to the very processes by which people select careers in education.[3] In other words, one of the professional expectations of prospective teachers is a substantial measure of independence. The norms governing how teachers should behave are "permissive" rather than "mandatory." Individual teachers are free to choose between cooperation and privacy. Unsolicited help is regarded as a breach of this prevailing norm structure. The overarching convention, according to Lortie's respondents, is "live and let live, and help when asked."[4]

A variety of mechanisms conceivably are available to teachers interested in helping each other. Collegial evaluation, for example, has been touted as a productive alternative to administrative "snoopervision." Lortie has indicated that teachers are very concerned about their effectiveness, but somewhat uncertain about how to assess it.[5] Gage suggests that a teacher can benefit from inviting a trusted peer to conduct a mass interview with students toward the end of a course.[6] The information gained from the interview is reported back to the colleague in a way that encourages instructional improvement.

Several Stanford researchers reported on a pilot test of a collegial evaluation program emphasizing the improvement of classroom teaching.[7] Working in tandem, teachers selected their own evaluation criteria, observed each other teach, provided each other feedback, and developed plans of assistance. On the whole, the 30 participants reacted favorably to the program, finding it adaptable to their particular circumstances.

In a somewhat different, but related venture, teachers in Toledo, Ohio, are experimenting with collegial supervision.[8] A small cadre of veteran Toledo teachers are involved in advising and supervising 32 newly hired teachers through regular classroom visits and follow-up meetings. At year's end, the veteran teachers will evaluate the rookie teachers and the results will largely determine whether they are rehired. The veteran teachers are given a 1,000 dollar bonus above their regular salary and are relieved of their teaching duties. The Toledo plan was the product of a collaborative effort by the local school system and the teachers union. While national teacher unions remain skeptical about the program, Toledo educators are laudatory.

The use of veteran teachers as intern supervisors has also been initiated, though in a less far-reaching way, in Florida, Georgia, and

Oklahoma. A spokesman for the National Education Association has observed, however, that the further spread of such programs is constrained by mandatory collective-bargaining laws in many states.[9] These laws prohibit teachers from being involved in hiring and firing decisions concerning fellow union members.

Few constraints exist to prevent teachers from helping each other plan and instruct, however. Team teaching and team planning received considerable publicity during the sixties, when open education and open-space schools garnered national attention. By pairing up or forming larger groups, teachers could assume greater responsibility for coordinating the instruction and classroom management of a relatively large number of students. In addition, teachers were afforded a chance to determine the curricular areas in which they were most interested or well-versed and, presuming there was a sufficient distribution of interests and talents in the team, allowed to focus on their preferences. Teaming seemed particularly attractive to elementary teachers, who traditionally were so tied down with fulltime supervision of their classes that they had little time to meet individually with students, go to the bathroom, or take a coffee break.

In recent years as talk of "burnout" has increased and teacher mental health has become a major educational concern, teacher support groups have been recommended as a worthy objective for self-help efforts. Teachers are urged to meet periodically and discuss candidly their anxieties about job loss, fears of student behavior problems, stress over increasing job demands, interpersonal conflicts with supervisors, and the like. Open sharing of problems with peers is supposed to reduce the likelihood of destructive internalization of dissatisfaction. Hearing that other teachers experience similar concerns can minimize the sense of personal failure and isolation. In one of the few systematic studies of the impact of teacher support, Nancy Isaacson found that "support was a contributing, but usually not a determining factor in subjects' decisions to remain in or to leave the teaching profession."[10]

While support groups may provide a useful opportunity for teachers to air grievances and anxieties, professional development activities focus on personal growth. Teachers can contribute to their own development and that of colleagues in a variety of ways. They can visit schools where teachers are trying innovative programs. They can conduct needs assessments and plan workshops in areas where increased skill is desired. Over the last decade, teachers even have created their own Teacher Centers to serve as places where colleagues can meet, work, and learn together without being supervised by administrators. A recent review of exemplary Teacher Center programs in *Education Week* (October 13, 1982, p. 7) listed a variety of imaginative enterprises, including a Staff Development Academy in Jefferson County, Colorado. Three full-time staff members apprise 400 full-time teachers of the latest education research. These 400 teachers, in turn, pass the new material on to their 4,600 colleagues in the district. In addition to these activities, state and local affiliates of the two major teacher unions regularly schedule conferences and workshops where teachers are paid consultant fees to share ideas with and provide training for fellow teachers. Ironically, one of the topics in greatest demand at these workshops and conferences in the early eighties has been career alternatives to teaching![11]

The potential benefits of greater teacher involvement in professional development are numerous. Some teachers, for instance, report that teaching peers allows them to refine their own skills. In addition, they receive the adult recognition and feedback on performance so often missing in the classroom. Several studies suggest that teacher participation in planning school improvement activities is related to school effectiveness and favorable student attitudes.[12] Professional development also may provide a source of supplementary income for veteran teachers close to the top of the salary scale. In Lincoln, Nebraska, for example, a cadre of full-time "master teachers" earns extra money for designing and teaching curriculum-related inservice courses to colleagues.[13]

Obstacles to Self-Help

Despite some promising developments in various parts of the country, it seems clear that teachers are unable alone to provide a sufficient amount of assistance to prevent continued problems with their profession's health.

A number of reasons exist to help explain why self-help efforts cannot completely offset the negative forces currently threatening the profession. One reason is simply the fact that fewer bright young teachers are moving into teaching. As a result, a traditionally vital wellspring of new ideas, energy, and enthusiasm has been slowed to a trickle. Fewer new teachers also has meant that veterans are deprived of opportunities to pass on their experience-based wisdom. One Palo Alto teacher admitted that sharing her wisdom with acolytes had been a major source of professional pride to her—one that could not be matched by interactions with age-mates. With the mean age of Palo Alto teachers hovering around fifty, she no longer had much opportunity to pass on her accumulated professional wisdom.

A second reason why teacher self-help is not completely meeting the need concerns teachers themselves. The fact is that many teachers, after years of low pay, low status, and public criticism, have simply resigned themselves to their fate. Playing the victim's role, they complain but do little to improve the situation. They convince themselves that no amount of effort will make a difference. They sadly feel that they have few skills to share and little knowledge worth imparting to colleagues. A study of teachers in five California high schools dramatized the growing sense of apathy.[14] Fewer than half of the teachers interviewed took advantage of opportunities to participate in school decision making, even though such participation might have led to job improvements and greater satisfaction.

While the absence of large numbers of new teachers and flagging teacher initiative certainly discourage self-help efforts, probably the major reason why teachers do not provide more assistance to each other is the organizational structure of schools. The argument is that schools are organized in ways which make it difficult for or actually prevent teachers from working closely with colleagues.

Take the authority structure of most schools, for example. The authority structure encompasses the processes by which school decisions are made and the individuals who are officially recognized as participants. In the previously cited California study of school decision making, a major reason why many teachers refrained from participation was their feeling that involvement in decision making would not assure influence.[15] In other words, they believed that no matter what they contributed to the process, ultimately the principal, superintendent, or board of education would determine the course of action. Given this fact, a majority of the teachers preferred to spend their time in their classrooms. The important point of the study, however, was that teachers wanted to participate in making school decisions—if only their involvement constituted more than a token gesture.

A major attraction of the Teacher Center movement was the fact that teachers typically were invested with authority for running the centers and planning their professional growth activities. Unfortunately, cuts in federal aid to education during the Reagan administration have forced many Teacher Centers to close. Dashed expectations resulting from policy shifts of this kind make it increasingly difficult to engage teachers in self-help programs.

Another difficulty with trying to generate greater teacher involvement is the fact that teachers with a desire to exercise leadership generally have faced two basic choices—become involved in union activities or prepare for building administration. If they opt for the latter alternative, teachers may feel it necessary to maintain a "low profile," hoping that they will not be regarded as troublemakers by those who ultimately are responsible for selecting new administrators.

Teachers who have been vociferous champions of teacher causes may not be selected as principals by boards of education.

A second aspect of school organization that works against self-help efforts concerns control structure. The control structure of a school subsumes various mechanisms for ensuring that district objectives are accomplished—rewards, sanctions, teacher evaluation, and supervision. As indicated earlier, the fact that evaluation of teacher performance serves as an official basis for decisions to retain or release teachers has undermined attempts to promote collegial evaluation. Teachers are compelled to regard evaluation as a threatening rather than a growth-oriented process. Union representatives express discomfort with the idea of assessing peer performance when the possibility exists that these evaluations will be used by administrators.

The process by which new teachers are socialized to teaching in conjunction with the way space and time are allocated in schools further serve to inhibit teacher efforts to help each other.[16] Most schools consist of cubicles in which individual teachers work alone, removed from contact with colleagues. Because of tight scheduling, time is rarely available in sufficient quantity to permit intensive interaction among teachers during the regular school day. Support groups, collegial evaluation, supervision of rookies by veteran teachers, professional development, and team planning all require substantial investments of time. Lortie has concluded that from an individual's earliest days as a teacher, he or she learns to rely basically on personal resources:

> Anxiety is increased by the limited support teachers receive in the demanding early months . . . they turn to others for help, preferring the informal exchange of opinions and experience to reliance upon the hierarchy. But the cellular organization of schools constrains the amount and type of interchange possible; beginning teachers spend most of their time physically apart from colleagues. Beginners receive more supervisory attention from principals and others, but . . . it rarely amounts to more than a few hours a month. Since the beginner spends so much of his time away from other adults, it falls upon him to discern problems, consider alternative solutions, make a selection, and, after acting, assess the outcome.[17]

Strength in Numbers

Teachers have learned the hard way that they can do relatively little to help themselves as long as they act individually, in pairs, or even as faculties. As a result of the school district consolidation movement and the growth of governmental control over education, authority for schooling has grown increasingly more centralized. To protect their interests, teachers have formed unions—the two largest being the National Education Association and the American Federation of Teachers. Currently about three-fourths of American public-school teachers belong to unions.[18]

Over the years, these unions and their affiliates have won a number of victories designed to improve the job of teaching. Improvements have centered on salaries, benefits, and more recently, working conditions. Teachers now earn much more than they once did. They enjoy such benefits as health insurance, retirement plans, sick leave, and life insurance. Cooperative purchasing plans and credit unions are available in many districts.

In an effort to improve working conditions in schools, unions have negotiated agreements concerning maximum class size, teacher safety, and teacher evaluation procedures. Grievance procedures exist so that teachers are assured of opportunities to express their concerns and due process. Procedures have been negotiated for recruiting and selecting teachers, choosing and reimbursing advisors for extracurricular activities, entering material into personnel files, and dismissing tenured teachers. Legal and financial assistance often are available from union headquarters for teachers whose jobs are threatened.

Many of these gains have been made possible as a result of the unions' successful campaign for collective bargaining. Some form of collective bargaining now is available in 38 states.[19] More than 1,400 of the nation's 16,000 school districts bargain collectively. In a study of six districts around the United States, Susan Moore Johnson found that collective bargaining can help teachers without undermining administrative authority or promoting a "work to rule" mentality.[20] Further, the advent of collective bargaining has meant greater job security for many teachers.

An additional benefit of teacher unionization has been increased political clout. Representing almost three million teachers, the NEA and AFT constitute powerful forces during elections. In 1974, for example, 91 percent of the candidates endorsed by the New York State United Teachers were elected. Nationwide, four out of every five pro-education candidates won, typically with the assistance of local, state, and national unions.[21] By supporting pro-education candidates with funds and volunteer labor, the unions have worked to preserve the hard-fought gains of the past few decades. As in any contest, though, gains are rarely possible without incurring costs. In addition, despite the unions' power, evidence exists that they currently are losing ground.

Backsliding into the Eighties

Union rhetoric notwithstanding, it is difficult to proclaim that the teacher unionization movement and spread of collective bargaining have been unqualified successes. Sarason, in an assessment of the movement, has concluded:

> It [teacher union movement] has won a number of benefits for teachers, but these gains have not made for more satisfied teachers. Indeed, in a number of instances union gains have produced polarizations within a school system, and between the system and the community, that have lessened the levels of job satisfaction.[22]

There are other sources of concern besides increased polarization. The issue of teacher salaries is illustrative of current union problems. Earlier it was noted that teacher earnings have failed to keep pace with inflation. Richard Wynn, in a recent analysis of income data for teachers, finds that between 1960 and 1979 the ratio of average U.S. teacher salaries to U.S. per capita income declined substantially.[23]

During the period of rapid growth in collective bargaining in public education teacher earnings actually appear to have lost ground to those of the general population! Of course, the argument can be made that the gap in earnings would have been even greater had collective bargaining not existed. Wynn reports, however, that teacher salary gains in states characterized as *intensive* collective bargaining states (where 67 percent or more of K-12 teachers are represented at the bargaining table) were not significantly different from those in unintensive collective bargaining states (where 33 percent or fewer of K-12 teachers are represented at the bargaining table). He concluded,

> There is no evidence, on the basis of data included in this study, to indicate that collective bargaining has had a positive influence on teacher salaries over a sustained period of time.[24]

If financial security is one leg upon which a union stands, job security is the other. Here, again, teacher unions are in trouble. The various forces of retrenchment, outlined in Chapter 4, have combined to chip away at the rolls of teacher unions. Large-scale Reductions in Force (RIFs) have taken place despite union resistance. In San Francisco, the failure of the local AFT chapter to prevent mass firings led to its defeat and replacement by an NEA affiliate. Traditionally unions have opposed renegotiating contracts in order to preserve jobs, but in the eighties as the recession deepens many teachers are accepting lower salaries in order to keep themselves and colleagues working.

The inability of unions to ensure the financial or job security of their members is a danger sign for those who would attach their hopes exclusively to teachers helping teachers. As teachers are RIFed, union membership drops, thus depleting coffers and reducing the resources available for lobbying efforts. The election of Ronald Reagan in 1980 and the gains made by Republican candidates for Congress are clear proof of the diminished political influence of pro-public-education forces. No friend of public school teachers, Reagan has pressed for tuition tax credits, a move that would benefit private and parochial schools. In 1982 he declined to address the national convention of the NEA in Los Angeles, an affront that few Presidents would have risked in the past.

Other indications exist that teacher unions are losing ground. The single salary schedule, long a central plank in union platforms, is being abandoned by some school districts in order to permit officials to offer higher salaries to science, mathematics, and vocational education teachers. To cut costs, negotiated benefits such as sabbaticals and tuition reimbursements are being eliminated. Teachers are compelled to accept larger class sizes and assignments for which they feel inadequately prepared. Even seniority and tenure—perhaps the most sacred of union tenets—are under attack. School officials claim that merit, not length of service, should determine who continues to work when jobs are cut.

Debates over how school districts should effect savings and staff reductions are dramatizing the fact that teachers themselves are split on a number of issues. Some teachers feel that seniority and tenure too often protect incompetent colleagues, thereby demeaning the profession. Certified social studies teachers in post-Proposition 13 California, for example, were hardly pleased when they were "bumped" by elementary teachers with but a year's seniority. In one California high school, RIFing and within-district transfers based on seniority resulted in a six member mathematics department with no certified mathematics teachers![25] It is predictable that as educational resources become more scarce, competition and disagreements between colleagues will intensify, thereby diminishing the capacity of unions and other professional groups to provide effective assistance to all members. Signs of negative competition were present in a recent study of three New York City high schools in the aftermath of budget cuts.[26] Teachers reported interdepartmental friction over differences in class sizes, textbook allocations, room assignments, and student assignments.

In-fighting among teachers also was evident at the 1982 national convention of the American Federation of Teachers. A bitter, racially charged debate resulted when union leaders pressed for passage of a resolution supporting the union's efforts to overturn a Boston court ruling ordering the layoffs of white teachers to preserve the jobs of black teachers. The resolution finally passed, but black delegates were enraged and criticized white leaders for backing down on past commitments to affirmative action.

A vivid illustration of the failure of teachers to collaborate effectively is the running battle between the NEA and the AFT. Though their interactions are less acrimonious than in past years, the two groups show little likelihood of merger—despite the obvious political advantages to be gained. Efforts to merge the two groups in New York State during the sixties aborted after a few years, evidence that local and regional jealousies take precedence over matters of overall professional importance. In 1980, the NEA endorsed Jimmy Carter for President, while the AFT supported Edward Kennedy. The fact that both groups backed losers is probably the most potent testimony to the contemporary influence of the teaching profession.

By 1983, the NEA and AFT were squaring off on two key educational issues for teachers: seniority and merit pay. While the AFT continued to support seniority, the NEA filed a brief supporting affirmative action in a reverse-discrimination suit before the Supreme Court.[27] On the other hand, while the NEA steadfastly opposed merit pay schemes, Albert Shanker of the AFT took a position of qualified support.[28]

Sensing growing infighting and vulnerability of teacher unions, a number of critics have begun to push for reforms that would permanently weaken the capacity of teachers for collective action. Myron Lieberman, once a proponent of teacher bargaining, and Thomas Shannon, executive director of the National School Boards Association, both have urged the dismantling of collective bargaining.[29] A group calling itself Concerned Educators Against Forced Unionism has been formed to work against provisions requiring non-union members in union schools to pay dues.[30] In a number of states elected officials are working on legislation to prevent teachers from striking. These officials apparently can count on strong public support for their efforts. The 1982 Gallup Poll found that 79 percent of the national sample favored compulsory arbitration.[31]

Unable alone to offset the combined forces of economic retrenchment and political conservatism, not fully prepared to join together in common cause, teacher unions and their membership face years of continued challenge and disappointment. As more energies are channeled into "bread and butter" issues and sheer survival, less activity is likely to be directed toward improvements in schools and the job of teaching. Policymakers must wonder about the possibilities of attracting new teachers to a profession mired in such uninspiring matters. The next chapter confronts the possibility that teaching—at least as it is currently known—may not survive the eighties and explores possible corrective courses of action for educational leaders.

Part IV

Adversity as Impetus for Improvement

CHAPTER 9

R_x for the Teaching Profession— Euthanasia or Rejuvenation?

This book opened with the contention that the profession of teaching—especially that segment which staffs urban and rural public schools—is threatened to an unprecedented degree. Of more than passing historical interest is the fact that other professions—such as law, city planning, public administration, nursing, librarianship, and social work—also have fallen on hard times. Seymour Sarason's work describing the growing malaise among many professionals in the United States has been used to develop the conceptual framework for the book.[1] Sarason attributes the malaise in part to discrepancies between how professionals are trained and what they *expect* to do on the one hand, and what they actually do within the circumscribed reality of the large organizations that increasingly serve as their work settings, on the other. The book is addressed in part to educational policymakers, in the hope that their periodic deliberations regarding the "state" of public schooling can be expanded to include a thoroughgoing analysis of ways to improve teaching conditions.

As the argument in the preceding chapters unfolded, it was maintained that the job of teaching has undergone a complex series of changes, changes leading to increased task ambiguity and insecurity. The lack of consensus about how to improve working conditions only has served to exacerbate the problem. Changes in students— some possibly perceived, others all too real—add to the difficulties. Complaints from the public always have attended teaching, but recent years have witnessed a growing number of legal, legislative, and procedural constraints to back up the complaints. The impact of these constraints often has been the deprofessionalization of teaching.

To make matters worse, when teachers seek assistance, they increasingly encounter "organizational" problems similar to those they face on the job. Teacher educators and researchers are constrained by the pressures of large colleges and universities—tight budgets, performance evaluation, accountability demands, and so on. Government agencies pushing for innovations and reform frequently become mired in their own paperwork and politics. Even teacher unions and associations have behaved like big organizations at times and failed to respond effectively to the concerns of a troubled profession.

The systematic nature of the analysis in this book may suggest to some that data are being manipulated to create the illusion of crisis. Many can cite examples, of course, of schools and teachers that are succeeding, even under the most adverse conditions. It is not my intention to demean the dedication and noble efforts of these educators or to imply that the teaching profession may disappear overnight. Ironically, perhaps, it is precisely because of the daily heroics of veteran teachers who refuse to give up that this book was written. A profession is likely to die slowly and painfully, losing status, public support, and new recruits. At each step along this course, examples of professional commitment and effectiveness may be sought and publicized in order to motivate those "in the trenches" and forestall public panic. By the time the citizenry becomes aware of the true condition of the profession, it may be too late. Too few talented new professionals will be prepared to replace retiring veterans. A growing percentage of jobs will go to those lacking in skills and/or employment alternatives. Dedicated and aging veterans watch as the ranks fill with well-intentioned, but inept or minimally committed newcomers.

If policymakers cannot assist teachers in rejuvenating their profession, the crisis will most likely surface first in urban high schools. Skeptical readers are invited to set aside this book and go talk with teachers who work in these settings. In my travels to urban schools across the United States, I hear the same concerns, the same sense of alarm. Teachers feel overwhelmed, anxious, on the verge of losing control. Teachers are overwhelmed by expectations that grow annually, even as school budgets decrease. Good teachers are capable of dealing with periodic crises. What is harder to manage is the constant uncertainty, never knowing when confrontations will arise or teaching positions will be eliminated. No different from other workers who find themselves facing uncertainty year in and year out, teachers eventually find the psychic toll too great and look elsewhere for employment.

Given the variety of threats and the particularly precarious position of segments of the profession, a reasonable question to ask may be, "Should the teaching profession be allowed to deteriorate further and possibly die?" Euthanasia may well be the best prescription if teachers no longer are able to fulfill the vital functions expected of them. To *decide*, after probing inquiry and debate, that the teaching profession is outdated would be a conscientious course of action. What seems unconscionable, though, is to ignore the need for such deliberation and simply permit the profession to wither and die of neglect.

DOES TEACHING STILL FULFILL VITAL FUNCTIONS?

To hear many critics talk, the impact of doing away with teachers would be minimal. As previously mentioned, some scholars suggest that teachers make little difference in the lives of students, especially when compared to the influence of family background and socio-economic status. What would happen if professional teachers were no longer available to staff public schools?

The demise of the teaching profession would not necessarily lead to the shutdown of schools. After all, schools could still be staffed by other kinds of workers—computer technicians, paraprofessionals, custodians, law enforcement officials, or some yet-to-be-defined group. If teachers—or other individuals systematically trained to structure learning opportunities for students—were no longer available, what might be the impact?

It seems unlikely that the situation would revert to that which characterized American society prior to the development of the teaching profession. In that earlier era, essential knowledge and skills were imparted in the home and church and on the job, for the most part. The process was somewhat arbitrary and unsystematic in many cases, and large segments of the population—including the poor, young women, and nonwhites—received little or no formal instruction. Today these groups are more assertive concerning their right to an education. In addition, the nature of the knowledge needed to survive in the twentieth century is such that its informal acquisition is unlikely to be very effective.

An argument can be made that young people could acquire the necessary instruction through computers and other technological devices. Several problems arise, however. These machines are often expensive and, therefore, not equally accessible to all students. Also, a certain amount of prerequisite learning and intelligence is required to be able to comprehend and utilize instructional technology.[2] Questions concerning the safety and maintenance of costly machines also occur. What would prevent students from vandalizing equipment? Finally, some subject matter—in areas such as study habits, the arts, character development, and social interaction—may not be as appropriate for computerization as mathematics and reading.

"Glorified babysitter" is a derisive term sometimes employed to describe teachers. If teaching ceased to be viable, another issue that would need to be addressed concerns who would supervise young people. Computers are notoriously ineffective at supervision. The parents who claim public school teachers are nothing more than babysitters often have the financial resources to place children in private schools. Were teachers as they are now known to become obsolete or were public schools no longer able to attract fully professional teachers, these same parents still would be able to locate educational alternatives. The question is, What would happen to the children whose parents lack adequate resources?

The teaching profession serves as a bulwark against the widening of divisions which threaten to separate American society into islands of hostility. Few question the existence of these divisions. At the same time, it also is clear, though, that these divisions could grow even wider. Teachers and schools may not be able to bring about a fully integrated society, but they may well be preventing students from growing up totally unaware of the existence of people from other races and cultures. Teachers assist youngsters who lack other options to acquire the knowledge needed to share in the benefits of the society. That these youngsters may not always acquire this knowledge or actually achieve economic independence as adults is not necessarily an indictment of schools or teachers. A variety of factors—ranging from unstable home situations to discriminatory hiring practices—conspire to undo even the best efforts of the educational system.

There is a final sense in which the teaching profession is vital. Without teachers, it would be difficult to locate a group of comparable size which is so disposed to work for the benefit of the young. Pediatricians help the young, but they do not interact with them regularly. Parents obviously are concerned, but frequently they are too close to their children or too ego-involved in parenting to function as effective instructors. Besides, the active interest of parents in the young may not extend beyond their own children and their children's friends. By virtue of their concern for and daily contact with large groups of young people, teachers are unique. It is unclear that several million replacements with similar sensitivities and motivations could be enlisted to work with the young were teachers to disappear. After all, if such replacements existed in requisite abundance, this book would not be called for in the first place. Additionally, it is unlikely that the domestic scene will shift so dramatically that parents will be able to assume greater responsibilities for the young.

Working with the young, however, is no longer revered by large segments of the population. Fewer adults opt to have children. Those who do frequently find it difficult or unsatisfying to raise them. More families are characterized by two working parents, and many adults seem to be more concerned with their own growth than that of their offspring. Senior citizens, who make up an increasingly large percentage of the population, now compete for resources once earmarked for the young and express their desire to live in "adult" communities free of children. In fact, those with children today are frequently the victims of housing discrimination, restricted to age-segregated ghettos in unattractive sections of town.

Given the emerging adult-centered ethos of the eighties, the need for trained professionals to work with young people on a daily basis actually seems to be greater, rather than less. The need also exists for organized groups of these professionals to serve as youth advocates, contesting for increasingly scarce resources with spokesmen for "adult" interests. The days when funds for the young were "hands off" to politicians and interest groups are over.

If the case can be made that professional teachers offer unique services to the society—services that are essential to its future wellbeing and which cannot be replaced by machines or less-skilled workers—the issue that then must be addressed is what has to be done to remove current threats to the viability of the teaching profession. The remainder of the book addresses this issue. The intention is not to record the last word on ways to rethink the nature of teaching, but instead to inaugurate a serious and ongoing dialogue about how to improve life for American educators.

THE REJUVENATION OF TEACHING

A variety of solutions for problems associated with school staffing are plausible. Some, for example, may advocate greater governmental intervention, perhaps leading to the creation of an educational equivalent of the Public Health Service for understaffed schools. The Teacher Corps, in fact, served in a similar capacity until it fell victim to budget cuts by the Reagan administration. A national education system might even be a consideration under a different President.

Those who oppose greater governmental intervention counter that an answer can be found in expanded opportunities for free enterprise. Tax credits and vouchers in theory would stimulate constructive competition in the public sector, eventually leading to more rewards for effective teachers. Such schemes invariably offer greater potential benefits to teachers of higher ability students. Little assurance exists that the law of supply and demand would function any more equitably in education than it has in other sectors. Those who start with the most resources are likely to finish with the most resources.

Greater governmental intervention or increased free enterprise in education are strategies that are likely to require a tremendous mobilization of resources. There also is no guarantee that either will address directly the two over-arching concerns of this book—unrealized teacher expectations and deteriorating conditions of teaching. If the current crisis in teaching has a positive dimension, it may lie in the opportunity to confront these concerns in imaginative new ways. Crises can be desirable occasions for innovation, since dire circumstances generally mean there is less to lose by taking risks.

The fundamental choice for policymakers is whether 1) to alter the preparation of teachers sufficiently to minimize the likelihood of unrealistic expectations or 2) to change the job of teaching sufficiently to maximize the likelihood of teacher expectations being realized. While the latter course of action is the more creative and promising, it is unlikely that current policies defining the work done by teachers can all be changed at once. Therefore, some combination of the two strategies probably is justified.

What follows is a possible scenario for teachers and policymakers that combines elements of both strategies. The intention is to suggest a comprehensive set of changes that may forestall further disillusionment by teachers while providing impetus for improvements. The heart of the prescription involves reconceptualizing the job of teaching, but it would be unrealistic to pretend that such a change could be effected without a variety of other changes. These include alterations in existing policies, recruitment procedures, rewards, working conditions and sources of support for teachers. Conveniently, and with some historical precedent, these suggestions may be referred to collectively as the "Eight R's":

1. Reassess national, state, and local priorities
2. Remunerate teachers better
3. Recruit more talented teachers
4. Reduce constraints on teachers
5. Reconceptualize the job of teaching
6. Reorganize schools
7. Revise educational research agenda
8. Redesign teacher training programs

It is encouraging to note that policymakers are already beginning to act in a number of these areas. An attempt thus will be made in the remaining pages to highlight recent indications of increased concern and improving conditions for teachers. Caution, however, is urged against over-generalizing on the basis of scattered promising signs. The major work of rejuvenating teaching still lies ahead.

Reassess Priorities

Advocating a reassessment of national, state, and local priorities may be perceived as a time-worn exercise in futility—a process certain to foster waste and inertia. There are several reasons why previous efforts to shift priorities may, in fact, have failed to generate bold new policies.

First, the ethos of affluence that prevailed after World War II may have mitigated against thinking seriously about priorities. The feeling that there was enough to go around for everyone tends to distract people and prevent them from working responsibly on the delineation of priorities. Times have changed, however. As resources become scarcer, competition intensifies.[3] Senior citizens and childless adults begin to vie with youth advocates for revenues. Parents of handicapped children compete with parents of normal children. Public school people contend with nonpublic school people. Higher education officials fight with representatives of local educational authorities. Under such circumstances, thinking about priorities is not only realistic, it is essential.

Past efforts to develop public priorities have approached the task from the standpoint of which functions, amidst diminishing resources or increasing demands, should continue to be provided and at what level. The public typically has not been fully apprised of the functions that no longer would be undertaken as a result of policy shifts and subsequent redistribution of resources. An effective strategy may be to specify to those affected—in this case the people served by the schools—exactly what can no longer be done if resources are redistributed. When such a strategy was implemented on a small scale in San Jose, California, following Proposition 13 budget cuts, parents at one city high school were told that the resulting loss of personnel meant teachers no longer could call home to check on absent students, strangers could not be prevented from visiting the campus, corridors could not be supervised, and teachers would be unable to counsel students individually.[4] So concerned were parents when they heard exactly what budget cuts would mean that they flocked to the next School Board meeting and demanded the reinstatement of lost teaching positions. Their effort succeeded!

The lesson is that simply arguing that education must be a high priority rarely produces active support. People need to understand alternative priorities and the likely impact of a shift in priorities.

If a persuasive case for greater support for schools—and ultimately for teachers—is to be made, it is also important to help taxpayers see schools as resource-generating, rather than resource-consuming, institutions. They must be shown that a key to the productivity, morale, and growth of any modern society is the quality of the education it receives. That the Japanese are both a very literate and a very productive people is no coincidence. Neither is it coincidental that teachers are highly valued members of Japanese society.

One of the factors that may impede a quick shift of priorities in the United States is the pervasive sense of despair with which many adults regard the future. Until recently, Americans virtually worshipped the future. Life was always getting better. More recently, though, people have come to believe that each new year brings only a diminution in the quality of life—scarcer resources, a more polluted environment, greater world instability, and less earning power in terms of real dollars. Characterized by pundits as the "me" generation and the "culture of narcissism," adults manifest a strong desire to make the most of the moment. Perhaps the ultimate rejection of the future is the decision by many adults to have no children. Any era in which the future ceases to be attractive is likely to be one in which schools—which are premised on the very idea of growth and progress—will suffer.

If American society were ever in need of a mission, the time is now. Restoring the public's faith in the future would be a worthy contender for top priority. Schools not only stand to benefit from a concerted drive to make the future a source of hope and inspiration again, they would be essential to the accomplishment of such a mission. Schools may not be able to eliminate all the threats to security and quality of life that presently tarnish the public's crystal ball, but they at least have the potential to spawn the attitudes, competence, and values necessary to keep people working toward a better world. It is hard to imagine, on the other hand, how emasculating public schools and allowing the teaching profession to grow further disenchanted can foster anything resembling longterm progress.

One way to commence the process by which priorities can be delineated may be to consider what disturbs people about today's youth. Teachers are not the only ones to feel that young people are different now. Crass materialism, lack of commitment to causes greater than the individual, poor communications skill, and abuse of drugs are only some of the troublesome characteristics found in contemporary youth culture. What are adults prepared to do to prevent succeeding generations from being similarly characterized? More importantly, what positive traits are desired for the young? Cooperation, responsibility, imagination, problem solving ability, dedication, tolerance, fairmindedness—these and other vital qualities are unlikely to be acquired incidentally. They must be modeled, learned, and practiced. Churches used to provide a firm grounding in many of these areas, but the recent rise of the Moral Majority and intolerant fundamentalism suggests that organized religion may be playing more of a divisive than an integrative role in American society. Schools and teachers are prepared to respond to the challenge, but only with a clear mandate from the public, support from government at various levels, and sufficient resources.

Encouraging indications exist that the time for rethinking the role of public schooling is opportune. The downward slide in Scholastic Aptitude Test scores has been arrested. Gains in achievement have been made by black students in particular. Narrow notions of what is "basic" education are giving way to broader, more realistic conceptions of what will be needed by citizens of the twenty-first century. At least 25 bills were introduced during the 79th Congress to upgrade science, mathematics, technology, and foreign language teaching.[5] Greater collaboration between the business community and public schools signifies growing recognition that the country's economic future is inextricably linked to the talents of the young.

Public opinion polls provide additional cause for optimism. The downward trend in the public's rating of the schools has been reversed.[6] The public seems more interested in increasing federal support for education than other sectors, such as defense and social services.[7] Of particular relevance for teachers is the fact that, if cuts do have to be made in school spending, the public strongly opposes reducing the number of teachers and increasing class sizes in order to effect these cuts.[8]

As the 1984 Presidential election approaches, definite signs exist that education and the fate of teachers are becoming campaign issues. President Reagan, for example, has endorsed merit pay for teachers. Democratic challengers have been courting teacher groups and advocating higher salaries for teachers.

Politicians have been joined by higher education officials. In February 1983 an unprecedented meeting took place at Yale University. Chief state school officers from 38 states and the presidents of more than 40 of the nation's leading colleges and universities met to explore ways to attract more academically able people into teaching. Participants agreed that "a climate now exists to mount a broad national attack on the pervasive problems of the prestige, power, pay, and preparation of America's schoolteachers."[9]

Remuneration and Recruitment

If it is possible to establish the education of the young as a national and state priority, then a concerted effort can be made to provide teachers with a more competitive wage and thus increase the chances for a steady flow of high quality persons to the profession. Chapter 2 presented statistics to indicate that such measures will be necessary if American schools—particularly those in urban and rural areas— are to be adequately staffed once the present, aging cohort of teachers retires or opts to leave teaching. Higher salaries alone, of course, are no guarantee that bright, committed individuals will be attracted to teaching. Other changes, to be addressed shortly, must occur in order to increase the likelihood of a stable workforce for the public schools of the next century. Higher salaries, though, can serve as a powerful magnet to contemporary college students considering various career options and a concrete symbol of the public's regard for education and teachers.

The difficulty with recruiting and holding talented teachers is obvious when people who handle garbage, gasoline, and groceries can earn more than those who work with young minds. Some school districts already have acknowledged the problem and initiated special programs. Houston, Texas, is an example.

Houston's Second Mile Plan was developed following a study that linked high teacher turnover to poor student performance.[10] Teachers receive stipends for working in schools in disadvantaged areas and in schools for the handicapped and juvenile offenders. Monetary incentives also are used to recruit teachers in subject matter areas such as mathematics, physical sciences, and vocational education— areas where critical shortages of qualified teachers are beginning to be experienced. There even is an allocation in the program to give extra pay to teachers with outstanding attendance and to teachers who help recruit other teachers into the district. During the first two years of Second Mile—from 1979 through 1980—approximately eleven million dollars was paid to two-thirds of Houston's 10,000 teachers. The maximum stipend that any teacher can earn in a year is $3,500.

In Boston, Superintendent Robert Spillane has initiated a new program to raise the instructional standards of teachers.[11] While part of the effort involves dismissal proceedings for teachers judged to be incompetent, cash awards will be made for instances of outstanding teaching. The Boston Teachers Union has supported most aspects of the new program, including the idea of dismissing incompetent teachers.

Another recent development in teacher remuneration is pressure for differential pay for individuals in certain subject matter areas. In 1982 the National Commission on Excellence in Education heard testimony urging higher salaries for mathematics and science teachers.[12] Participants seriously doubted if sufficient recruits in these areas could be attracted without more competitive salaries.

Teacher organizations have opposed pay schemes such as differential salaries based on subject matter area and the Second Mile Plan, contending that money should go instead to raises for all teachers. Unfortunately, the failure of the teaching profession—for the reasons previously discussed—to continue to attract individuals of uniformly high competence and commitment has meant that all teachers may not deserve more pay.

One alternative to special stipends, "combat pay," merit bonuses, and other incentives being introduced in urban districts across the country may be a two-track staffing arrangement. One track would be reserved for individuals with outstanding qualifications who are committed to teaching as a career. One-third to one-half of the positions in a school might be set aside for these master teachers. Positions would be tenureable, following a probationary period, and rewarded, perhaps, at twice the current salary teachers receive. An assumption underlying this scheme is that schools may not be able to fill every opening with an exemplary, career-oriented teacher, but they probably could fill at least half their openings with such individuals. Senior master teachers might even be eligible for one of several "endowed chairs" in each school. These chairs could be underwritten by local businesses and professional organizations.

The second track in this system would be reserved for individuals who either lacked the outstanding qualifications deemed appropriate for master teachers or the commitment to teaching as a career. In this group might be included very able people with a definite contribution to make—recent college graduates still undecided about a career, persons in other occupations desiring a different experience for a few years, and senior citizens nearing retirement. Teachers in the second track would be hired on the basis of non-renewable three-year contracts. This provision would assure a steady flow of new ideas and talents into schools and clearly separate career teachers from others. The salary for temporary teachers would correspond to current teacher salaries. Working in the second track could serve as an opportunity for some individuals to evaluate whether or not teaching was the appropriate career for them. Such a scheme might not cost much more than many districts are currently spending to maintain faculties where almost everyone is located near the top of the salary schedule.

Vance and Schlechty, on the other hand, express doubt that any new salary scheme which would attract and hold 10 percent of the upper 50 percent of college graduates could be afforded. They maintain,

If policy makers wish to exclude the bottom quarter of the bottom half of college graduates from the talent pool, they must pay the price for attracting the top half. That price is substantially higher than most legislators seem to be willing to acknowledge.[13]

Robert Scanlon, Pennsylvania's Secretary of Education, feels that legislators can be pressured into improving teacher remuneration.[14] If State Education Departments deliberately create teacher shortages by mechanisms such as raising the standards on skills tests required for teacher certification, Scanlon argues that local school districts will be forced to compete for available teachers by offering higher salaries. An ad hoc committee of the Council of Chief State School Officers has endorsed this kind of plan.

The fact that policymakers at various levels are talking seriously about the need to rethink teacher remuneration and recruitment policies is encouraging. The basic thesis of this book, however, should be stressed again. Salary improvements or cash incentives alone are unlikely to resolve all the problems currently confronting teachers. These changes can be characterized as "first order changes." Arthur Blumberg and William Greenfield have provided a useful review of the limitations of first order changes. They state,

First order changes involve the rearrangement or substitution of parts of a system without disturbing the fundamental structure of a system. When first order changes are the basis of new programs, the results may indeed achieve some illusions of basic change. What is left untouched, however, is the framework through which people conceptualize their tasks and their relationships with others.[15]

The remaining recommendations are intended to go beyond first order change and alter the nature of the "system" within which teachers work.

Reduce Constraints

Among the additional changes necessary to rejuvenate the profession is the reduction of constraints which threaten to "deprofessionalize" teaching. Chapter 5 discussed some of these constraints and their origins. They encompass legal and legislative requirements, laws, and procedures as well as fiscal controls, accountability measures, and competency tests. While many of the constraints have been intended to upgrade the quality of schooling, their collective impact may have been just the opposite. Faced with a steadily growing set of regulations and rules, creative teachers often react by leaving the profession or, at least, the public schools. They resent the fact that the regulations and rules frequently are promulgated in order to discourage poor practice by a relatively small group of incompetents. They do not appreciate, for example, being required to attend workshops on classroom management when only a few teachers are unable to maintain orderly environments. Developing policy "by the worst example" discredits the good work of the majority of teachers and adds to the ethos of routinization and conformity which increasingly characterizes public schools.

Sarason's analysis of the dilemma of being a professional in the second half of the twentieth century has particular salience. Recalling the discussion in Chapter 1, he contends that college students seek professional careers in part because of the belief that they will be able to exercise personal judgment in the solution of challenging problems:

> It used to be that highly educated, professional people viewed themselves, and were viewed by others, as an elite fortunate in that they experienced work as fulfilling, challenging, and worthy, possessing few or none of the stifling characteristics of labor. Job dissatisfaction was not their problem, but that of the factory worker, clerk, and others in simple, routine jobs.[16]

As more professionals spend their lives working in large, bureaucratically organized settings, however, the gap between expectations and reality grows wider. No longer is it reasonable for budding young professionals to expect to function autonomously. The work professionals now perform involves less judgment, creative problem solving, and autonomy and more internalization of organization norms, formalization, and observation of guidelines. The message conveyed by these developments is straightforward and ego-devastating—everyone is dispensable. Regulations are designed to be followed by virtually anyone. Organizations simply look for individuals who will abide by the rules. Individuality, creativity, and personal judgment cease to have the high value they once were accorded. Compliance becomes the cardinal virtue.

Frederick McDonald addressed these issues in testimony submitted to the House Committee on Education and Labor. Among the challenges facing education that he cited were the following:

> . . . we need to know how to organize the social and professional life of large numbers of knowledge workers (including teachers). These knowledge workers are most effective in organizations; but, they have been educated for independence and initiative. Many of them presently feel

constrained by the demands of an organization for cooperation, integration, and interdependence among knowledge workers. Also, such knowledge workers need a variety of incentives in addition to economic ones. The knowledge worker must have a challenge, opportunity to use his knowledge in what he regards as desirable ways.[17]

Teachers, like others, derive satisfaction from feeling indispensable. This source of satisfaction has been steadily diminished—the victim of job reduction and job simplification, prescriptive laws, the growing spectre of legal liability and malpractice suits, and seniority rules. Innovations aimed at reducing or simplifying the tasks of teaching tell teachers they are not perceived to be intelligent enough to manage complex operations. Prescriptive laws tell them they are not trusted by the public and its representatives. The threat of lawsuit and its financial burden tell them that conformity is a safer, if not more satisfying, course of action. Seniority rules tell them that factors other than talent and training are valued as a basis for determining who will keep his or her job.

Educational policymakers are beginning to realize what law enforcement officials long have known. More laws do not necessarily produce improved performance. Sometimes just the opposite may be true. Reducing the total number of regulations and rules can foster more productive organizational climates and actually increase the likelihood that the most essential guidelines will be enforced consistently. Treating teachers like professionals will not ensure that schools will accomplish all that is expected of them, but it may have a greater chance of success than more coercive strategies.

While policymakers have stepped up efforts to regulate the quality of people entering the teaching profession, there are promising signs that the trend toward increased regulation of practicing teachers is being reversed. Regardless of the motives behind them, moves by the Reagan administration to reduce federal regulations may cut down on teacher paperwork and unnecessary supervision. The shift in funding procedure to the "block grant" is likely to eliminate many of the "strings" attached to prior categorical aid programs. A shift even can be detected in recent Supreme Court decisions regarding teachers. Victor Rosenblum notes that the Supreme Court's support for professionalism is waxing:

> By according deference to decisions based on professional judgments and inviting and utilizing empirical data to substantiate or reject officials' rationales for their decisions, the Court may be criticized by some for failing to provide judicial leadership. But these complex norms that accord judicial

recognition and incentives to educators' bona fide skills and concerns are more likely to enhance the equities and efficacies of education than judicially imposed ideologies.[18]

Removing some of the constraints that teachers perceive to be so inhibiting could eventually stimulate greater trust between the profession and the public and reduce the high degree of politicization that has characterized contemporary school systems. As a result, teachers may not be compelled to devote so much time and energy to lobbying, legal defense, and mobilization of support efforts. With teachers possibly having more time available for "professional" concerns, the focus of this discussion can shift from contextual matters to the nature of the job itself.

CHAPTER 10

Reconceptualizing the Job
of Teaching

Education is heir to a seemingly never-ending succession of fads and short-lived innovations. Despite the constancy of change, there are certain aspects of the education enterprise which steadfastly remain the same. In *The Culture of the School and the Problem of Change*, Seymour Sarason takes a look at some of the stable characteristics of schools—or what he refers to as regularities.[1] Regularities tend to be the things that are so commonplace that they are taken for granted. Exceptions, of course, can be found for any regularity, but they are readily recognized as "exceptions." Researchers and practitioners often overlook regularities in their quest for changes and improvements because they seem such a fixed part of operations. An example of such a regularity would be the five-day, Monday-through-Friday school week.

The device that Sarason cleverly utilizes to reveal regularities in schools is the hypothetical visitor from another planet. Presumably intelligent but unfamiliar with the behaviors or motives of American educators and students, the visitor tries to make sense of its new surroundings by searching for patterns, repeated behaviors, and the like. Nothing is taken for granted, since it has no prior set of conceptions to interfere with what it sees.

The focus of Sarason's visitor's observations tends to be school organization and culture rather than the job of teaching. If, however, the visitor were to concentrate its attention on enough teachers for a long enough period of time, it is certain that some definite patterns would emerge. These regularities must be recognized and understood before any substantial effort can be made to explore alternative conceptions of teaching.

EVER THUS A TEACHER

Perhaps the first observation that an interplanetary visitor would make would be that the big people who stand or sit in front of lots

134

of little people tend to do so for most of the time they are in the facilities we refer to as schools. Relatively little interaction occurs between big people. If observations were made over a period of a few years, it would also be noted that the big people rarely have contact with the same little people for more than a year. And if the observer were particularly patient and spent a half century or so investigating schools, he would see that an older big person does essentially the same things with the ever-changing groups of little people that he did when he was just beginning to work.

Observations such as those above may help us to realize that teaching is one of the few professions where an adult is called on to spend an entire career doing essentially the same work in the same setting with constantly changing groups of immature clients. If we were asked to design a profession that would maximize the likelihood of frustration and discontent, we could not do a better job.

As lawyers and physicians grow older, in contrast to teachers, they often are able to reduce caseloads and spend more time consulting with other, younger practitioners. Contacts with clients frequently continue over a number of years, permitting practitioners to get to know clients well. Collegial interactions take place on a regular basis and focus on problem solving and other substantive matters.

Inspired by the visitor from another planet, we may begin our own search for regularities and the insights they spawn.

It quickly becomes apparent that most teachers rely on essentially the same "tools of the trade." For example, they tend to employ questions as a basic instructional device. In fact, it is even difficult to imagine an entire class period in which no questions are asked.

Those familiar with how schools are operated also know that there is little official or public encouragement of diversity among teachers. In fact, conformity and observation of standard procedures are rewarded much more often than acts of creativity, individual judgment, and unusual achievement. The way students typically are assigned to teachers illustrates the conformist norms operating in schools. Rather than matching the unique characteristics of particular students with the unique talents of particular teachers, school officials typically assign students in arbitrary ways. The implication is that a teacher is a teacher is a teacher—all no more than interchangeable parts of the educational production process.

The profession itself even reinforces the image of virtuous conformity by reserving praise for those who *survive* until retirement, rather than for teachers who manifest special talents or accomplish challenging pedagogical tasks along the way. Teachers are socialized to think of themselves exclusively as teachers, rather than teacher-biologists, teacher-historians, teacher-child development specialists, or teacher-researchers. Teachers are rarely regarded as leaders except in the context of their classrooms. Those who wish to exercise leadership often feel they must seek administrative positions. Few school administrators ever voluntarily return to teaching.

The culture of the American school serves to reinforce the notion that there is, to paraphrase David Tyack, "one best teacher." Educational researchers have abetted this unitary conceptualization by distilling observations of thousands of teachers into sets of "common characteristics" of *the* effective teacher. They suggest that schools will be better places for students if all teachers simply adopt—in herdlike fashion—the traits of this idealized artifact of correlational analysis. Perhaps the next step will be to determine the characteristics of the ideal student. Then it might be possible for schools to work on turning out identical copies.

The absence of a variety of conceptions of effective teaching probably is as much a comment on American society as it is a statement about the lack of imagination within the education community. Americans always have experienced difficulty differentiating between the kind of individualism that permits public servants to help determine how they best can provide service, given their particular strengths, and the kind of individualism that produces navel-contemplating parasites on the public payroll. Willing to tolerate nonconformity in private industry, entertainment, and sports, Americans fail to see the benefits that acknowledging individual differences might have for teaching. As a result, schools are typically staffed to avoid deviations from the norm, rather than to attract unusual talent and strengths.[2] Such a policy mitigates against the recruitment and retention of exceptional teachers.

In summary, the way the job of teaching is conceptualized is desperately in need of reassessment and imagination. Robert Kahn's indictment of the design of industrial work could just as easily be directed at teaching:

> Too long, managements have believed that fragmenting jobs into mindlessly small units of work will lead to increased production. Too long, unions have believed that they could protect workers from extreme hazard and physical stress, but not from being bored to death. Too long, society at large has assumed that there is no such thing as psychological pollution. We have comforted ourselves with the mistaken belief that workers slough off the effects of monotonous, meaningless jobs when they leave their factories and offices for home and community.[3]

Kahn goes on to make a brief for the "humanization of work," and while he speaks primarily of factory work, his recommendations could serve as criteria to guide a reconceptualization of teaching— a process to which we turn next:[4]

> I define the humanizing of work as making work more appropriate and fitting for an adult to perform. By this criterion, humanized work:
>
> 1) should not damage, degrade, humiliate, exhaust, or persistently bore the worker;
>
> 2) should be interesting and satisfying;
>
> 3) should utilize many of the valued skills the worker already has, and provide opportunity to acquire others;
>
> 4) should enhance, or at least leave unimpaired, the worker's ability to perform other life roles—as spouse, parent, citizen, and friend, for example;
>
> 5) should pay a wage sufficient to enable the worker to live a comfortable life.

NEW NOTIONS OF TEACHING

Decision theorists contend that the likelihood of selecting the most appropriate course of action is maximized by considering the greatest number of alternatives. Systematic reviews of alternative conceptions of teaching are rare, however. Teaching is what it is largely as a result of public expectations and accumulated pedagogical traditions. The problem with such a process is obvious. How can we know that the way teaching currently is conceptualized is best unless we consider other alternatives?

One reason why a reassessment of the job of teaching has failed to occur may be that policymakers keep asking too narrow a range of questions. Perhaps, for political reasons, they feel that expressing concern for any component of the education enterprise other than students creates too great a risk of alienating taxpayers. It is acceptable to raise questions about the quality of working conditions for coalminers, assembly line workers, and nuclear engineers, but not teachers. Until recently policymakers were more likely to ask, "How can we make teachers do what they are expected to do?" than "How can the job of teaching be made as exciting and rewarding as possible?"

The following exploration of alternative ways to think about teaching is offered in the spirit of the latter question. The intention is not to present *the* alternative, but merely to suggest some different ways to conceptualize and deliver instructional services. The following ideas are not sequenced in any particular order nor are they all necessarily compatible.

What if we stopped acting as if there were one best type of teacher and began valuing diversity? Such a change ultimately might make it easier for us to value different types of learners as well. One reason why teachers may be disturbed by the recent proliferation of panaceas (Chapter 3) is not the lack of consensus, but the fact that they feel pressure to find the right one. If the value of diversity in teaching were acknowledged by policymakers, teachers might regard new approaches to teaching more positively.

Perhaps teachers should be spending more time assessing their different strengths and matching them with the strengths of particular students.[5] This kind of change in teaching would necessitate changes in school organization, to be sure, For instance, the notion of a "class" as an organizational unit would have to be rethought. Constituting classes on the basis of student age—one of the most pervasive "regularities" in American education—would seem to be incompatible with efforts to match particular teachers with particular students.

The fact is that there is no approach to teaching that has been shown to be uniformly effective for all ages of students or all subjects. Bruce Joyce and Marcia Weil, in *Models of Teaching*, provide an indication of how many different ways exist to conceptualize what teachers do.[6] If teachers value individuality as much as Lortie has suggested, providing greater encouragement for the development of unique teaching styles may induce more talented teachers to remain in the profession.[7]

What if teaching were conceptualized as a set of complex technical skills, including problem solving, hypothesis testing, decision making, information processing, logical analysis, and resource allocation? Some teachers may be bothered by what they perceive to be a personal lack of technical skills. They may point enviously to physicians and engineers because their professions entail a "technical core." In fact, teaching, too, entails skills, but policymakers often fail to regard teaching as more than a craft—a collection of routine practices.

To reinforce the notion of teaching as a set of sophisticated technical skills, it may be necessary to move away from the current subject matter orientation of schools. Curricula, especially in secondary schools, tend to be rooted in the disciplines such as biology, mathematics, and sociology. Emphasis is placed more on the acquisition of information than skills or competence. Today, particularly in light of the spread of microcomputers and early exposure of the young to mass media, the conventional information-imparting function of teachers may be somewhat outmoded. It may make more sense to conceptualize teaching as a process whereby professionals certify that students have completed certain experiences and acquired certain skills. Mastery learning programs are based on such a conception and reports of their success may prompt increased interest in the technical dimension of teaching.[8]

Instead of or in addition to courses such as algebra II or american history, teachers also might begin to construct learning experiences in, say, measurement or conflict resolution. In this way students could start to recognize the existence of key "generic skills" that cut across disciplines and occupations. Jerome Bruner, in a recent article, notes the emerging interest in "metacognition"—teaching people to think about their own thinking, how to think about problem solving, how to attack problems.[9] Is it inappropriate to envision teachers providing instruction in "thinking?" Learning experiences such as those just cited may better be offered as intensive workshops running all day for four weeks than fifty minute classes in the traditional sense. For years, Fork Union Military Academy in Virginia, for example, has offered students one intensive course at a time and found the innovation to be well-received.

What if a tack somewhat opposite to the preceding one were considered? Teachers would be regarded as discipline-based scholars as well as instructors. Years ago, for example, chemistry teachers considered themselves to be chemists. Staffing schools with teacher-child development specialists, teacher-historians, teacher-linguists, and other teacher-academicians could foster greater self-respect among teachers and upgrade their public image. Possibly, such action might also help bridge the gulf now separating public school teachers from professors. For such a reconceptualization to be effective, teachers, like their college counterparts, would need released time to conduct their own scholarly inquiry and research. It is likely that the process by which teachers are credentialed would have to be altered as well.

So far the implication has been that teachers would work only with the young. What if part of a teacher's time was spent teaching adults? Teachers might be offered flexible schedule options permitting them to teach late afternoon or evening courses. Under certain conditions, adults from the community might be allowed to come to school during the day and take classes along with younger students. Such an innovation could combat immature conduct in classrooms by providing multiple adult role models. Offering classes to both young students and adults also would reduce age segregation—a disturbing and rapidly increasing fact of life in the United States. Teachers might welcome the chance to interact with adults during the day.

Under certain circumstances, teachers actually may be more effective teaching parents to teach their children than directly teaching the children themselves. This suggestion may be particularly appropriate where drill and practice or patient listening to recitation is required.

What if students came to school with questions and teachers helped them find answers? As noted earlier, the opposite is much more likely to occur. Teachers ask questions, and students are expected to provide the answers. This process, it could be argued, reinforces passivity on the part of learners. Perhaps students should be exposed to different situations, tasks, experiences, and problems and directed to generate questions that need to be answered. Learning to ask the right question can be as important as learning answers to standard queries, particularly given the constantly changing state of knowledge.

In order for such a shift in pedagogical practice to take place, teachers would have to modify their traditional role of inquisitor. This change would likely necessitate modifications in the way student performance is evaluated, since questions constitute the basis for most testing and formal assessment.

Teachers might become more like coaches.[10] Coaches do not rely much on asking questions, yet they often manage to elicit outstanding performances from their players. Coaches give directions and provide structured opportunities for individuals to acquire experience. Players are permitted to learn by trial and error and from peers. When they have questions, they turn to the coach, who typically provides answers or directions on how to find answers.

Coaches learn to capitalize on special moments. The environment in which coaches work has not been so risk-proofed that such special moments—or epiphanies as May Sarton might say—are unlikely to arise. Coaches work with volunteers and thus are relieved of the responsibility of totally eliminating risk. Perhaps there are ways in which teaching can become more of a voluntary contract between teacher and learner, thus providing teachers with some of the motivational leverage that coaches enjoy.

A key difference between the classroom and the playing field or performing stage is the fact that what occurs on the latter cannot be predicted—there is an ethos of excitement about it. One fundamental problem with contemporary schooling is that the experience is essentially the same for large numbers of students. The satisfaction of doing something extraordinary is denied the vast majority of students and, as a result, teachers. Some of the most effective instruction I have ever witnessed took place during Outward Bound survival training. It is difficult to describe the enthusiasm that results when individuals who have believed themselves incapable of adapting to unfamiliar, often harsh surroundings discover they can learn wilderness skills. Outward Bound instructors point out that no two courses are ever the same.

Some of the reasoning behind the suggestion that teaching might become more like coaching was expressed in a prescient essay by Nelson Foote. The occasion for Foote's pronouncements was a series of hearings on the creation of a National Institute of Education conducted in the early seventies by the House Committee on Education and Labor. The volume of testimony, including Foote's piece, was entitled *Alternative Futures in American Education*. It still stands as one of the few relatively systematic efforts to think about changes in the role of teacher. Foote wrote as follows:

> . . . teaching depends as much on the teacher's understanding the particular nature of the learner as on possessing the knowledge to be transmitted. . . .
>
> The study of the individual student by the teacher is neither widely nor intensively practiced in schools of any kind. Ironically, it is explicitly recognized and honored most where it is probably needed least, in primary schools, where children are in fact less differentiated from each other in their development than at any later period of their lives. In general, students tend to be classified into groups roughly corresponding with age, the members of which are homogeneous enough to justify exposing them simultaneously to the same selections of knowledge. Any further adaptation of content to match the unique qualities of individuals tend to occur without plan during the interaction of student with teacher or with other students. Yet in the art of matching content with learner over time lies most of the raison d'être of teaching.
>
> Although not widely practiced in schools, some very advanced examples of elaboration of the role of the teacher as a guide in personal development exist. The best known of these examples is coaching in any field of artistic or athletic performance. Here the emphasis, after the acquisition of basic technique, is no longer on the imparting of knowledge but on the improvement by practice in its use.[11]

What if teachers at age 55 did not have to perform the same functions that teachers perform at age 22? At present, the way the job of teaching is conceptualized fails to note stages of adult development—physical, emotional, and cognitive. To assume that most 22-year-old teachers have the wisdom of 55-year-olds or that the latter possess the energy of the former is ridiculous, however.

Alonzo Crim, Superintendent of the Atlanta, Georgia, schools, wonders whether the wisdom of older teachers cannot be put to better use by engaging them as discussion leaders rather than fulltime classroom instructors.[12] For example, these individuals could be invited into classrooms to conduct seminars on the Great Books, to consult with students doing research papers, and to engage individuals in Socratic dialogue. Freed of the large group instruction and classroom management duties of younger teachers, veteran teachers would have opportunities—if they wished—to reflect on their prior experiences and refine their scholarly talents. It is too easy these days to forget that many people enter teaching because of a genuine love for learning. Too often—under present conditions—they discover there is precious little time for their own continued academic growth.

Careful analysis of the relationship between age and teaching tasks may well indicate that there exist certain optimal ages for certain kinds of teaching. Adding economic and psychological considerations to the analysis may produce further factors that should be taken into account by those responsible for staffing schools. For example, it may be that teaching is a profession for the very young and the very old. The temperaments of individuals in their thirties and forties may not be suitable for working with the young. They may not be able to afford to teach, even with the increased remuneration prescribed earlier. If it were possible to provide these teachers with opportunities to perform non-instructional tasks or earn extra income during the years when they need it most, they might be less inclined to abandon careers in teaching altogether.

The ideas presented so far have concerned the tasks of teaching. What if changes were made in staffing patterns as well? In Chapter 9, a two-track scheme was mentioned as a possible means to encourage talented teachers to stay in the profession. Teachers might also be rotated through a variety of positions in order to minimize boredom and stimulate the acquisition of new skills. Unlike the prevailing educational career model, though, teachers would be expected to return to the classroom. Currently, if a teacher becomes an administrator, he or she is unlikely to go back to teaching voluntarily. Even if the ex-teacher wished to return, such a decision would be difficult, given the salary structure in most school systems.

What if teachers knew when they were hired that they would periodically shift from a classroom assignment to another type of position, such as supervisor, administrator, adjunct professor in a four-year or community college, or even student? The rigors and emotional demands of teaching might seem much less enervating if teachers knew that every few years they would undertake a different set of responsibilities. The fact that some of these responsibilities would entail leadership activities might also serve to alleviate many of the status and power problems experienced by teachers. An arrangement somewhat like the one just described has been in place in New York City for several years and seems to be well-received by many teachers. By contract, New York teachers can opt for a non-classroom assignment after a designated number of semesters of regular teaching. Other school districts grant sabbaticals periodically, then expect returning teachers to spend a semester or two "on special assignment" in the central office sharing the knowledge acquired while on leave.

The preceding examples are only a few of the possibilities that might be explored during a thorough reassessment of the job of teaching. Nothing has been said of arranging for teachers to work with students for longer than a year, combining groups of teachers into professional teams, or clinical-tutorial models of teaching. Nothing has been said of moving to a more collegiate model, where teachers alternate between large lecture classes and small seminars. What is important at this point is not any particular idea but simply the fact that discussion and debate commence soon and that teachers be actively involved. Teaching *will change* in the coming decades. Given the dwindling supply of capable new teachers, changes in students, decreasing resources for schools, and rapid advances in technology, such an assertion seems justified. The only questions are whether or not the changes will be aimed at merely replacing or retraining teachers and who will determine the changes.

School Reorganization

Teaching takes place in an organizational context. In the future, perhaps schools will be replaced by other types of organizations. In any event, a discussion of changes in teaching must include an investigation of the impact of these changes on the organization of the workplace—which, for present purposes, will be referred to as a school.

Many of the possible changes presented in the preceding section entail alterations in the way teachers are assigned. The division of labor in most public schools seems designed more for the convenience of a few people than the maximization of teaching effectiveness. For example, new teachers often are assigned the most difficult groups of students or given multiple preparations without even a room to call their own.

Traditionally administrators and department heads determine who will teach what, when, and where. Reconceptualizing teaching may necessitate a new decision-making model, one in which the teachers themselves play a more active role in determining how subject matter areas will be covered and which students will be assigned to which teachers. Shared decision making will not eliminate all problems and disputes, but teachers will be less apt to resent assignments if they have helped to determine them. In fact, a simple rule to guide all school decision making might well be—no decision will be made without the involvement of those expected to implement the decision.

Thomas Sergiovanni has provided an excellent set of assumptions upon which to base efforts to increase teacher participation in school decision making:[13]

1. Teachers desire to contribute effectively and creatively to the accomplishment of worthwhile objectives.

2. The majority of teachers are capable of exercising more initiative, responsibility, and creativity than their present jobs or circumstances allow.

3. Supervisors should work to help teachers contribute their full range of talents to the accomplishment of school goals.

4. Supervisors should encourage teachers to participate in important as well as routine decisions.

5. The quality of decisions made will improve as supervisors and teachers make full use of the range of insight, experience, and creative ability that exists in their school.

6. Teachers will exercise responsible self-direction and self-control in the accomplishment of worthwhile objectives that they understand and have helped create.

Skeptics may point out that shared decision making requires considerable time. Time, they add, is expensive. There can be no disputing these assertions. On the other hand, few people advocate replacing our democratic form of government with a dictatorship, even though the latter may be more efficient. The point that many citizens—educators and non-educators alike—sometimes overlook is that there are other worthy values besides economy and efficiency. It is time to think seriously about the merits of organizing schools on the basis of values other than this pair borrowed from private industry.

A variety of organizational changes eventually may be required if schools are to be healthy, attractive places for teachers as well as students. Principals may need to function more as instructional leaders than managers.[14] Changes may be needed in the reward structure and in evaluation strategies. What happens to a teacher's problem when it arises may have to be reviewed. Too often teachers are left to deal with problems on their own. Alternatives to conventional classes need to be considered, along with the archaic systems by which academic credits are calculated.

Just as there is no "one best teacher," there is no "one best school organization." Different conceptions are needed of the organizational context in which teaching takes place—different decision making processes, different divisions of labor, different control structures, different mechanisms for coordinating activities. Farber and Miller have noted that teacher burnout is attributable "not only to overt sources of stress but often to unexamined factors within school structures that lead to a lack of a *psychological sense of community*— a lack which produces feelings on the part of teachers of both isolation and inconsequentiality."[15] The alternative school movement of the late sixties and seventies addressed many of these "structural" concerns and demonstrated that teachers as well as students may need alternatives.[16] Where will ideas for school reorganization come from? Perhaps educational researchers can utilize their talents to help inform educators of the range of alternatives available.

Revise Research Agenda

If the educational research community wishes to avoid further alienation from practitioners, it must begin to behave in more imaginative and constructive ways. Focusing scholarly skills on critiques of teachers and schools serves to demoralize those who must work with the young, discredit the teaching profession in the eyes of the public, and assist those who compete with education for resources. While no profession should be protected from systematic inquiry and evaluation, when investigative findings cease to be helpful to the subjects, the time has arrived for a revision of research agenda.

For researchers to be more credible in the eyes of practitioners, they must devote a larger proportion of their time to collaborative inquiry, joining with teachers and other educators in coinvestigative efforts to understand current concerns. In *Schoolteacher*, Lortie, in fact, calls for the development of cadres of teacher-researchers committed to working on classroom problems with university-based professors.[17] These joint efforts may not always lead to conceptual breakthroughs or sweeping new generalizations, since practitioners' concerns often are localized and idiosyncratic. Researchers can, however, help generate alternatives to standard practices, serve as planning consultants, and provide "consumer's guide" information on the relative advantages of competing programs and practices. A promising development in this area is the AFT's Educational Research and Dissemination Program.[18] After consulting teachers about problem areas where research might offer assistance, AFT staff members contacted well-known researchers and asked for help in identifying the best available studies. Research findings were translated into materials that teachers could read and apply. Cadres of teachers were selected and trained in the use of these materials. Once trained, these individuals became trainers of other teachers. The application of research findings by hundreds of teachers around the country provides an important opportunity for researchers and teachers to collaboratively validate existing studies.

Researchers have several important roles to play in any attempt to reconceptualize the job of teaching and reorganize schools. They can remind practitioners of historical precedents and inform them of practices in other places. Researchers can help design experiments to test the appropriateness of new ideas, collect information to assist practitioners in deciding on courses of action, and speculate on the future needs of students and society. For these and other functions to be appreciated by practitioners, though, researchers must learn how to relate to those who work in schools. Where researchers have been most successful, they have spent long hours observing and interacting with school personnel, shared impressions openly prior to their publication, demonstrated a willingness to modify these impressions in light of feedback from practitioners, and stuck around after studies were completed to discuss next steps.

An encouraging trend in educational research over the past decade has been the "school effectiveness" movement. What started out as an effort to 1) identify particular schools that were more successful with students than other schools having certain key similarities (i.e. size, location, student socioeconomic status) and 2) isolate unique features of the successful schools which could serve as guidelines for educational improvement, has turned into a joint effort by practitioners, professors, and policymakers to stimulate comprehensive school-based change. From Alaska to Wyoming, virtually every state in 1982 boasted some program designed to implement elements of school effectiveness research.[19] Efforts ranged from curriculum coordination and alignment projects attempting to make certain tests of student achievement reflect what teachers actually teach to training projects aimed at providing better instructional leadership. By focusing on schools rather than individual teachers, school effectiveness advocates acknowledge that the context in which teachers work is a critical element in plans for improving student learning.[20]

Redesign Teacher Education

Traditionally, the redesign of teacher education is one of the first recommendations to be made when critics zero in on the declining quality of schooling.[21] In the present set of prescriptions, however, it serves as the last recommendation. It makes little sense to alter teacher education until the preceding suggestions have been acted upon. How can new teacher education programs be designed until more is known about the functions that teachers-of-the-future will probably undertake and the settings in which they will work? Of what value would it be to train cadres of new teachers and send them out to schools organized along conventional lines? Long-time observers of the schools can testify to the problems which arose when teachers trained in "progressive" and "open" education programs accepted positions in traditional schools. The problem of unrealized expectations became acute.

Since systematic efforts to reconceptualize the job of teaching are but a proposal at this point, it is premature to speculate on substantive changes in teacher education. The possibilities are extensive. For instance, if future teachers are expected to spend more time helping students develop "generic" skills, teacher education programs may have to curtail their current emphasis on subject matter "methods' courses. If teaching comes to be regarded as more of a clinical process, greater exposure to the development of interpersonal and analytical skills may be needed. If opportunities for teachers to function as school leaders are expanded, more preparation in leadership skills will be necessary.

Until such time as a new conception of teaching becomes available to guide teacher educators, it would seem prudent to devote considerable time to providing prospective teachers with a clear idea of what teaching today actually entails. Reducing the discrepancy between preservice expectations and inservice realities can minimize teacher disillusionment. When "anticipatory socialization" programs dealing with the job realities of nursing were attempted by nursing educators, they were judged to be quite useful in improving rates of retention among nurses.[22]

Building a Healthy Teaching Profession

Americans, like people elsewhere, cherish their traditions, even those that no longer are realistic or useful. Images of the selfless, home-grown schoolmarm and the noble, if underpaid Mr. Chips are difficult to abandon, particularly during times when change has reached epidemic proportions. Ironically, as much as Americans complain about the quality of teaching in their schools, they are bound by ties of sentiment to past school experiences and particular teachers.

Despite the immediate comfort that comes from looking backward for solutions during periods of disquieting forward movement, such wistful recollections must be treated cautiously, particularly when they are brought to bear on policymaking. The days of stable neighborhoods when teachers were among the most highly educated members of a community are gone. Schools today are expected to handle a variety of social welfare tasks which traditionally were ignored or dealt with elsewhere. Many young people no longer come to school convinced of the value of an education or prepared to treat their teachers with respect. The complexity of teaching—along with the ambiguity of its objectives, the growing list of rules and regulations, and the insecurity of the job itself—hardly serves as an inducement to young people searching for a career.

The economic downturn that has characterized the early eighties may constitute more of an opportunity than a catastrophe for public education if it compels large numbers of talented recruits to consider careers in teaching because opportunities elsewhere have decreased. Policymakers, though, must be prepared for this possibility and make certain that the job of teaching is sufficiently attractive and challenging to hold these individuals once they have entered the profession. The real challenge of the next few years will be how to attract and retain talented new teachers, not, as some suggest, how to get rid of incompetent veterans.

In his insightful book *Two Worlds of Childhood: U.S. and U.S.S.R.,* Urie Bronfenbrenner suggests that one criterion by which a society may be judged is the extent to which it values and provides for its future generations.[23] How teachers are treated and regarded thus may be one useful indicator of how this society feels about the young. The imperiled state of today's teaching profession suggests that concern for future generations is not universally regarded as a high priority. History suggests that the prognosis for a society that becomes overly absorbed in immediate gratification and selfish, short-range concerns is not encouraging. Perhaps one reasonable step in restoring the public's faith in the future—and ultimately in itself—

would be to invest more energy, resources, and imagination in rethinking the mission of our public schools and the job to be done by those who spend more time with the young than anyone except (and sometimes including) their parents.

Notes

1. Domains of Disappointment

1. Seymour B. Sarason, *Work, Aging, and Social Change* (New York: The Free Press, 1977).

2. An excellent discussion of public concerns regarding various professionals is presented in Chapter 1 of Donald A. Schön's *The Reflective Practitioner* (New York: Basic Books, Inc., Publishers, 1983).

3. Sarason does discuss some implications of his work for teachers in "Again, the Preparation of Teachers: Competency and Job Satisfaction," *Interchange*, vol. 10, no. 1 (1978–79), pp. 1–11.

4. Sarason, *Work, Aging, and Social Change* (New York: The Free Press, 1977), p. 13.

2. Assessing the Vital Signs

1. *U.S. News & World Report* (October 20, 1980), p. 12. Evidence of a possible reversal of this trend was reported in *Education Week* (September 29, 1982). The lead article reported a slight improvement in SAT scores—two points on the verbal test, one point in mathematics. It is too early to determine if the increase will be sustained.

2. Jack McCurdy and Don Speich, "Drop in Student Skills Unequaled in History," *The Los Angeles Times* (August 15, 1976).

3. Nancy B. Dearman and Valena White Plisko, *The Condition of Education*, 1980 Edition (Washington, D.C.: National Center for Education Statistics, U.S. Government Printing Office, 1980), p. 87.

4. W. Vance Grant and C. George Lind, *Digest of Education Statistics 1979* (Washington, D.C.: National Center for Education Statistics, U.S. Government Printing Office, 1979), p. 33.

5. Ibid., p. 32.

6. *Phi Delta Kappan*, vol. 62, no. 2 (October 1980), p. 84.

7. Bruce K. Eckland, "College Entrance Examination Trends." In Gilbert R. Austin and Herbert Garber (eds.), *The Rise and Fall of National Test Scores* (New York: Academic Press, 1982), p. 30.

8. John Shelton Reed, *Available Evidence on Public Attitudes Toward Education* (Princeton, N.J.: Advisory Panel on the Scholastic Aptitude Test Score Decline, College Entrance Examination Board, 1977), pp. 30–31.

9. J.M. Stephens, The Process of Schooling (New York: Holt, Rinehart and Winston, 1967); James S. Coleman, *et al.*, *Equality of Educational Opportunity* (Washington D.C.: United States Government Printing Office, 1966).

10. John A. Centra and David A. Potter, "School and Teacher Effects: An Inter-relational Model," *Review of Educational Research*, vol. 50, no. 2 (Summer 1980), pp. 286–287.

11. Richard J. Murnane, "Interpreting the Evidence on School Effectiveness" (unpublished manuscript, 1980).

12. Michael Rutter, Barbara Maughan, Peter Mortimore, and Janet Ouston, *Fifteen Thousand Hours* (Cambridge, Mass.: Harvard University Press, 1979).

13. W.I. Thomas and E.S. Thomas, *The Child in America* (New York: Knoff, 1928).

14. *Education Week* (December 8, 1982), p. 3.

15. Frances Cerra, "Stress Buffeting Older Teacher Now in Schools," *New York Times*, October 14, 1980, p. B1.

16. *Phi Delta Kappan*, vol. 61, no. 4 (December 1979), p. 254.

17. R.C. Newell, "Teacher Stress," *American Teacher* (December 1978/January 1979), pp. 16–17; "Readers Report on the Tragedy of Burnout," *Learning* (April 1979), pp. 76–77.

18. "Teaching Teachers not to Teach," *Money*, vol. 9, no. 5, (May 1980), p. 90.

19. Anthony Gary Dworkin, "The Changing Demography of Public School Teachers: Some Implications for Faculty Turnover in Urban Areas," *Sociology of Education*, vol. 53, no. (April 1980), pp. 65–73. Joy E. Whitener, "An Actuarial Approach to Teacher Turnover" (Ph.D. dissertation, Washington University, St. Louis, Missouri, 1965). Whitener's findings were supported by W.W. Charters, Jr., "Some Factors Affecting Teacher Survival in School Districts" in Donald Gerwin (ed.), *The Employment of Teachers* (Berkeley: McCutchan Publishing Corporation, 1974).

20. Henry Levin, "A Cost Effectiveness Analysis of Teacher Selection" in Donald Gerwin (ed.), *The Employment of Teachers* (Berkeley: McCutchan Publishing Corporation, 1974).

21. Phillip C. Schlechty and Victor S. Vance, "Do Academically Able Teachers Leave Education? The North Carolina Case," *Phi Delta Kappan*, vol. 63, no. 2 (October 1981), pp. 106–112.

22. *Ibid.*, p. 112.

23. "Teacher Burnout: How to Cope When your World Goes Blank," *Instructor*, vol. 6 (1979), p. 57.

24. My appreciation to Sue Griffiths of Stanford University's School of Education for these data.

25. Schlechty and Vance, "Do Academically Able Teachers Leave . . . ," p. 108.

26. Wangberg, Elaine G., Metzger, Devon J.; and Levitov, Justin E. "Working Conditions and Career Options Lead to Female Elementary Teacher Job Dissatisfaction," *Journal of Teacher Education*, vol. 33, no. 5 (Sept/Oct 1982), pp. 37–40.

27. William H. McGuire, "Teacher Burnout," *Today's Education*, vol. 68, No. 4 (1979), pp. 5–7.

28. "Readers Report on the Tragedy of Burnout," p. 771.

29. Dworkin, "The Changing Demography of Public School Teachers . . . ," pp. 71–72.

30. Susan Walton, "Teacher Shortage in Math, Science Is Critical, Survey Finds," *Education Week* (March 31, 1982), p. 1.

31. "Teaching Teachers not to Teach," Money, vol. 9, no. 5 (May 1980), p. 90.

32. Dworkin, "The Changing Demography of Public School Teachers . . . ," pp. 67–68.

33. Alfred M. Bloch, "Combat Neurosis in Inner-City Schools," *American Journal of Psychiatry*, vol. 135, no. 10 (1978), pp. 1189–1192.

34. Nancy B. Dearman and Velena White Plisko. The Condition of Education 1980 Edition (Washington, D.C: National Center for Educational Statistics, U.S. Government Printing Office, 1980), p. 72.

35. *The Chronicle of Higher Education*, July 7, 1980, p. 8.

36. Thomas Toch, "New Statistics Indicate Supply, Not Demand, May Cause Teacher Shortages in This Decade," *Education Week* (May 19, 1982), p. 14.

37. George H. Gallup, "The 12th Annual Gallup Poll of the Public's Attitudes Toward the Public Schools," *Phi Delta Kappan*, vol. 62, no. 1 (September 1980), p. 11.

38. Stanley M. Elam and Pauline B. Gough, "Comparing Lay and Professional Opinion on Gallup Poll Questions," *Phi Delta Kappan*, vol. 62, no. 1 (September 1980), p. 47.

39. "Databank," *Education Week* (September 29, 1982), p. 12.

40. Jack McCurdy, "Job Outlook for Teachers Gains Quietly," *Los Angeles Times*. (July 20, 1980), p. 1.

41. Arni T. Dunathan, "Teacher Shortage: Big Problems for Small Schools," *Phi Delta Kappan*, vol. 62, no. 3 (November 1980), pp. 205–206.

42. Alex Heard, "Attracting and Keeping Good Teachers Is Serious Problem for Rural Schools," *Education Week* (October 19, 1981), p. 4.

43. Jack McCurdy, "Job Outlook for Teacher Gains Quietly," *Los Angeles Times*. (July 20, 1980), p. 18.

44. James W. Guthrie and Ami Zusman, "Teacher Supply and Demand in Mathematics and Science," *Phi Delta Kappan*, vol. 64, no. 1 (September 1982), p. 28.

45. Eileen White, "Sputnik at 25", *Education Week* (October 13, 1982), p. 11.

46. W. Timothy Weaver, "In Search of Quality: The Need for Talent in Teaching," *Phi Delta Kappan*, vol. 61, no. 1 (September 1979), pp. 29–32.

47. Victor S. Vance and Phillip C. Schlechty, "The Distribution of Academic Ability in the Teaching Force: Policy Implication," *Phi Delta Kappan*, vol. 64, no. 1 (September 1982), pp. 22–27.

48. Ibid., p. 25.

49. McCurdy, "Job Outlook for Teachers Gains Quietly," p. 19.

50. Schlechty and Vance, "Do Academically Able Teachers Leave . . . ," pp. 110–111.

3. Ambiguity and Insecurity

1. *Status of the American Public School Teacher 1975–76* (Washington, D.C.: National Education Association Research, 1977), p. 27.

2. Larry Cuban, "Persistent Instruction: The High School Classroom, 1900–1980," *Phi Delta Kappan*, vol. 64, no. 2 (October 1982), pp. 113–118.

3. For a provocative discussion of the relationship between multiple options and stress refer to Frederic F. Flach, *Choices* (Philadelphia: J. B. Lippincott Co., 1977).

4. Larry Cuban, "Teacher and Community," *Harvard Educational Review*, vol. 39, no. 2 (Spring 1969), pp. 266–270.

5. "Drive to Rescue America's Battered High Schools." *U.S. News and World Report*. (September 8, 1980), p. 47.

6. N.L. Gage, *Teacher Effectiveness and Teacher Education* (Palo Alto: Pacific Books, Publishers, 1972), p. 200.

7. Actually, to be entirely accurate, administrators have been "the last to go," with teachers coming second. See John Freeman and Michael T. Hannan, "Growth and Decline Processes in Organizations," *American Sociological Review*, vol. 40 (April 1975), pp. 215–228.

8. *Peninsula Times Tribune,* September 1, 1980, p. A-1.

9. Daniel L. Duke and Adrienne M. Meckel, "The Slow Death of a Public High School," *Phi Delta Kappan,* vol. 6, no. 10 (June 1980), pp. 674–677.

10. Carolyn Anderson, "The Search for School Climate: A Review of the Research," *Review of Educational Research,* vol. 52, no. 3 (Fall 1982), p. 400.

11. Beth Bond Supranovich, "Differentiated Staffing Revisited," *Phi Delta Kappan,* vol. 64, no. 1 (September 1982), p. 20.

12. Daniel L. Duke, Beverly K. Showers, and Michael Imber, "Teachers and Shared Decision Making: The Costs and Benefits of Involvement," *Educational Administration Quarterly,* vol 16, no. 1 (Winter 1980), pp. 93–106.

13. Daniel L. Duke, ed., *Classroom Management,* The Seventy–eighth Yearbook of the National Society for the Study of Education (Chicago: University of Chicago Press, 1979), p, xii.

14. For a description of these new roles, see Daniel L. Duke and Adrienne M. Meckel, "Disciplinary Roles in American Schools," *British Journal of Teacher Education,* vol. 6, no. 1 (January 1980), pp. 37–50.

15. For a detailed discussion of nine approaches to classroom management, refer to Daniel L. Duke and Adrienne M. Meckel, *Teacher's Guide to Classroom Management* (New York: Random House, 1984).

16. Albert Shanker, "Where We Stand," *New York Times* (May 18, 1981), p. E7.

17. Rhonda Barton, "Lost Jobs, Schools Aside, Massachusetts Coping." *The Oregonian* (October 24, 1982).

18. H.A. Wallin, *The Educational Employment Histories of the Professional Workplace in B.C. Schools, 1968–69.* (Vancouver: Centre for the Study of Administration in Education, The University of British Columbia, 1971).

19. James E. Bruno and Lynn Doscher, "Analysis of Teacher Transfers in a Large Urban School District" (Paper presented at the American Educational Research Association Conference, April 1979).

20. R.C. Newell, "Teacher Stress," p. 16.

21. Jack M. McCurdy, "Job Outlook for Teachers Gains Quietly," *Los Angeles Times,* July 20, 1980.

22. David B. Tyack, *Turning Points in American Educational History* (Lexington, Mass.: Xerox College Publishing, 1967), p. 413.

23. *Measuring Trends in Salaries and Wages in Public Schools: ERS Composite Indicator of Changes* (Arlington, VA: Educational Research Service, Inc. 1979), p. 3.

24. Thomas Toch, "Teachers Today Are Older, Poorer, and Much Less Happy With Career," *Education Week* (March 10, 1982), p. 13.

25. "1981–82 Salaries of School Professionals," *Education Week* (March 31, 1982), p. 14.

26. Dearman and Plisko, p. 76.

27. Grant and Lind, p. 76

28. Patrick H. Crowe, *How to Teach School and Make a Living at the Same Time* (Kansas City: Sheed Andrews and McMeel, Inc., 1978).

29. Judy Solkovits, "Salaries: Choosing Teachers from the Profession," *Education Week* (February 10, 1982), p. 18.

4. What's Happened to Johnny

1. Rudolf Franz Flech, *Why Johnny Can't Read* (New York: Harper, 1955).

2. Morris Kline, *Why Johnny Can't Add* (New York: St. Martin's Press, 1973).

3. Opal Moore, *Why Johnny Can't Learn* (Milford, Michigan: Mott Media, 1975).

4. Richard Stoller, *Why Johnny Burns His Schools Down* (New York: Vantage Press, 1978).

5. "Teacher Opinion Poll," *Today's Education*, vol. 69, no. 4 (November-December 1980), p. 8GE.

6. George H. Gallup, "The 14th Annual Gallup Poll of the Public's Attitudes Toward the Public Schools," *Phi Delta Kappan*, vol. 64, no. 1 (September 1982), p 46.

7. David Tyack and Michael Berkowitz, "The Man Nobody Liked: Toward a Social History of the Truant Officer, 1840–1940," *American Quarterly*, vol 29, no. 1 (Spring 1977), pp. 31–54.

8. G. Stanley Hall, *Adolscence* (New York: Appleton, 1904–5).

9. Statistics are reported in *Historical Statistics of the United States*, Part 1 (Washington, D.C.: U.S. Department of Commerce, U.S. Bureau of the Census, U.S. Government Printing Office, 1975), p. 368.

10. *Ibid.*, pp. 370–372.

11. Statistics are reported in *Historical Statistics of the United States*, Part 1 (Washington, D.C.: U.S. Department of Commerce, U.S. Bureau of the Census, U.S. Government Printing Office, 1975), p. 362.

12. David K. Cohen and Barbara Neufeld, "High School Education and the Progress in Education" (Paper presented at the Daedolus/St. Paul's Conference on Secondary Education, February 1981).

13. "Amid Discontent, Private Schools are Booming," *U.S. News and World Report*, vol. 87, no. 11 (September 10, 1979), p. 40.

14. Pamela Bardo, "The Pain of Teacher Burnout: A Case History," *Phi Delta Kappan*, vol. 61, no. 4 (December 1979), p. 252.

15. E.J. Kahn, Jr., *The American People* (Baltimore: Penguin Books Inc., 1975), p. 143.

16. "Now a School Problem: One-Parent Families," *The American School Board Journal*, vol. 167, no. 10 (October 1980), p. 19.

17. Kenneth Keniston, "Do Americans Really Like Children?" *Today's Education*, vol. 64, no. 4 (November-December, 1975), p. 18.

18. Ibid.

19. Brown shared his perceptions in an address on the American family delivered at the annual convention of the Confederation of Oregon School Administrators, June 24, 1982.

20. B. Frank Brown, "A Study of the School Needs of Children from One–Parent Families," *Phi Delta Kappan*, vol. 61, no. 8 (April 1980), pp. 537–540.

21. Kenneth Keniston, "Do Americans Really Like Children," p. 18.

22. Kahn, *The American People*, p. 77.

23. Daniel L. Duke and Adrienne Meckel, "The Slow Death of a Public High School."

24. Cheryl R. Perry, Adolescent Behavior and Criminogenic Conditions in the Culture of the High School (Ph.D. Dissertation, Stanford University, 1980), p. 161.

25. David Elkind, *The Hurried Child: Growing Up Too Fast Too Soon.* (Reading, Mass.: Addison–Wesley Publishing Company, 1981).

26. Diane Hedin and Dan Conrad, "Changes in Children and Youth over Two Decades: The Perceptions of Teachers," *Phi Delta Kappan*, vol. 61, no. 10 (June 1980), pp. 702–703.

27. Walter Doyle, "Are Students Behaving Worse Than They Used to Behave?" *Journal of Research and Development in Education*, vol. 11, no. 4 (Summer 1978), pp. 3–16.

28. Joan and Graeme Newman, "Crime and Punishment in the Schooling Process: A Historical Analysis" in Keith Baker and Robert J. Rubel, eds., *Violence and Crime in the Schools* (Lexington, Mass.: Lexington Books, 1980), pp. 14–15.

29. Judith P. Ruchkin, "Does School Crime Need the Attention of Policemen or Educators?" *Teachers College Record*, vol. 79 (1977), pp. 225–244.

30. Jack McCurdy and Don Speich, "Drop in Student Skills Unequaled in History," *Los Angeles Times*, August 15, 1976.

31. Dan Morgan, "Coming of Age in the '80s," *The Washington Post* (December 27, 1981).

32. Jan Norman and Myron Harris, *The Private Life of the American Teenager* (New York: Rawson, Wade Publishers, Inc., 1981).

33. Christopher Lasch, *The Culture of Narcissism* (New York: W. W. Norton & Company, Inc., 1978), p. 65.

34. Jeremy Seabrook, *What Went Wrong?* (New York: Pantheon Books, 1978), p. 26.

35. John M. Murray, "Narcissism and the Ego Ideal," *Journal of the American Psychoanalytic Association*, vol. 12 (1964).

36. Jan Norman and Myron Harris, *The Private Life of the American Teenager*, p. 127.

37. National Institute of Education, *Violent Schools—Safe Schools*, The Safe School Study Report to the Congress, volume I (Washington, D.C.: National Institute of Education, 1978), p. 5.

38. Daniel L. Duke and Vernon F. Jones, "Two Decades of Discipline—Assessing Recent Efforts to Reduce Student Behavior Problems" (Paper presented at the 1983 meeting of the American Educational Research Association).

39. "Teacher Opinion Poll," *Today's Education*, vol. 69, no. 3 (September–October 1980), p. 21 GE.

40. Alfred M. Bloch and Ruth Reinhardt Bloch "Teachers—A New Endangered Species?" in Keith Baker and Robert J. Rubel, eds., *Violence and Crime in the Schools* (Lexington, Mass.: Lexington Books, 1980), p. 82.

41. National Institute of Education, *Violent Schools—Safe Schools* (Washington, D.C.: National Institute of Education, 1978), p. 3.

42. *Ibid.*, p. 4.

43. Ibid., p. 2.

44. *A Report on Conflict & Violence in California's High Schools* (Sacramento: California State Department of Education, 1973), p. 5.

45. *Survey of Violence in Schools Occurring from 1964 Through 1968* (Washington, D.C.: U. S. Government Printing Office, 1970).

46. Sarnoff A. Mednick, "Primary Prevention of Juvenile Delinquency" in David Schichor and Delos H. Kelly, eds., *Critical Issues in Juvenile Delinquency* (Lexington, Mass.: Lexington Books, 1980).

47. J. Godwin, *Murder USA: The Ways We Kill Each Other* (New York: Ballantine Books, 1978).

48. Christine Alder, Gordon Bazemore, and Kenneth Polk, "Delinquency in Non-metropolitan Areas" in David Schichor and Delos H. Kelly, eds., *Critical Issues in Juvenile Delinquency* (Lexington, Mass.: Lexington Books, 1980).

5. COMPLAINTS AND CONSTRAINTS

1. Phillip C. Schlechty and Victor S. Vance, "Recruitment, Selection and Retention: The Shape of the Teaching Force" (Paper presented at the Research on Teaching Conference, Airlee House, February 1982), p. 10.

2. *Report of the National Advisory Commission on Civil Disorders* (New York: Bantam Books, 1968).

3. Arthur E. Wise, "Why Educational Policies Often Fail: The Hyperrationalization Hypothesis," *British Journal of Curriculum Studies*, vol. 9, no. 1 (1977), pp. 44–45.

4. A discussion of this case appears in Albert Shanker's column in the June 1, 1980, edition of the *New York Times*, p. 9E.

5. "Censorship in the Schools: Something Old and Something New," *Today's Education*, vol. 69, no. 4 (November–December 1980), pp. 56–60.

6. An excellent history and description of competency–based education can be found in Gene E. Hall and Howard E. Jones, *Competency–based Education* (Englewood Cliffs, N.J.: Prentice–Hall, 1976).

7. David Lisman, "Should Continuing Education Be Mandated?" *American Educator,* vol. 4, no. 2 (Summer 1980), pp. 30–31.

8. Thomas Toch, "N.C. Mandates Rating System for Educators," *Education Week* (October 12, 1981), p. 4.

9. Davis Lisman, "Should Continuing Education Be Mandated?" p. 29.

10. *Ibid.*

11. Susan Moore Johnson, "Performance-Based Staff Layoffs in the Public Schools: Implementation and Outcomes," *Harvard Educational Review*, vol. 50, no. 2 (May 1980), p. 233.

12. My appreciation to Walter Hathaway of the Evaluation Division, Portland Public School, for this information.

13. Data provided by the Confederation of Oregon School Administrators.

14. W. Vance Grant and C. George Lind, *Digest of Education Statistics 1979* Washington, D.C.: National Center for Education Statistics, (1979), p. 72.

15. A lengthy discussion of San Jose High is contained in Daniel L. Duke and Adrienne M. Meckel, "Slow Death of a Public High School," *Phi Delta Kappan*, Vol. 61, no. 10 (June 1980), pp. 674–677.

16. At one point not one of the six teachers in San Jose High's Mathematics Department was reported to be certified to teach mathematics.

17. Daniel L. Duke, Jon Cohen, and Roslyn Herman, "Running Faster to Stay in Place: New York City Schools Face Retrenchment," *Phi Delta Kappan*, vol. 63, no. 1 (September 1981), pp. 13–17.

18. Daniel L. Duke, "Environmental Influences on Classroom Management." In Daniel L. Duke, ed., *Classroom Management* (Chicago: The University of Chicago Press, 1979), p. 360.

19. Seymour B. Sarason, *Work, Aging, and Social Change* (New York: The Free Press, 1977).

6. How Helpful Is Higher Education?

1. B. Othanel Smith, "Pedagogical Education: How about Reform?" *Phi Delta Kappan,* vol. 62, no. 2 (October 1980), p. 87.

2. Timothy Weaver, "Projecting Teacher Needs and Professional Staffing Patterns for the mid-1980's" (Paper presented at the American Educational Research Association, 1980).

3. James Bryant Conant, *The Education of American Teachers* (New York: McGraw-Hill Book Company, 1963).

4. James D. Koerner, *The Miseducation of American Teachers* (Baltimore: Penguin Books, 1965).

5. *Ibid.*, p. 37.

6. Harry S. Broudy, *The Real World of the Public Schools* (New York: Harcourt Brace Jovanovich, Inc., 1972), pp. 64–66.

7. B. Othanel Smith, "Pedagogical Education: How about Reform?" front cover.

8. David C. Smith and Sue Street, "The Professional Component in Selected Professions," *Phi Delta Kappan*, vol. 62, no. 2 (October 1980), pp. 103–107.

9. Seymour B. Sarason, "Again, the Preparation of Teachers: Competency and Job Satisfaction," p. 10.

10. Beverly T. Watkins, "Schools of Education Tightening Programs in Response to Attacks on Teacher Training," *The Chronicle of Higher Education* (March 2, 1981), p. 1.

11. Thomas Toch, "Ed–School Group Urges Tougher Accreditation Standards," *Education Week* (September 29, 1983), p. 4.

12. Thomas Toch, "Teacher–Educators at Odds over National Accreditation," *Education Week* (March 3, 1982), p. 6.

13. For an excellent overview of the current state of inservice education in the United States, see *Education Week's* three–part series on the subject (September 29, October 6, and October 13, 1982).

14. National Education Association, *Status of the American Public School Teacher* 1975–76, p. 34.

15. S.J. Yarger, K.R. Howey, and B.R. Joyce, *Inservice Teacher Education* (In press).

16. Thomas Toch, "No Direction, No Accountability: Why the Inservice System Breaks Down," *Education Week* (October 6, 1982), p. 12.

17. Thomas Toch, "Inservice Efforts Fail a System in Need, Critics Say," *Education Week* (September 29, 1982), p. 10.

18. Thomas Toch, "Inservice Efforts Fail a System in Need, Critics Say," *Education Week* (September 29, 1982), p. 10.

19. Milbrey Wallin McLaughlin and David D. Marsh, "Staff Development and School Change," *Teachers College Record*, vol. 80, no. 1 (September 1978), p. 94.

20. Bruce R. Joyce, Clark C. Brown, and Lucy Peck, *Flexibility in Teaching* (New York: Longman, 1981).

21. Betty Dillon–Peterson, ed. *Staff Development/Organization Development* (Alexandria, Va.: Association for Supervision and Curriculum Development, 1981).

22. Thomas Toch, "New Ideas, New Programs Fuel Reforms in Staff Development," *Education Week* (October 13, 1982), p. 7.

23. An excellent review of contributions of research to practice can be found in J.W. Getzels, "Paradigm and Practice: On the Impact of Basic Research in Education." In Patrick Suppes, ed. *Impact of Research on Education: Some Case Studies* (Washington, D.C.: National Academy of Sciences, 1978).

24. Seymour B. Sarason, *The Culture of the School and the Problem of Change* (Boston: Allyn and Bacon, Inc., 1971), p. 48.

25. N.L. Gage, *Teacher Effectiveness and Teacher Education* (Palo Alto: Pacific Books, Publishers, 1972), p. 152.

26. Thomas Toch, "Researchers Ponder How to Reach Practitioners," *Education Week* (March 31, 1982), p. 4.

27. Roald F. Campbell, "The Professorship in Educational Administration—A Personal View," *Educational Administration Quarterly*, vol. 17, no. 1 (Winter 1981), pp. 12–13.

28. Kenneth Keniston, "Do Americans *Really* Like Children?" p. 20.

29. J.S. Coleman, et. al., *Equality of Educational Opportunity* (Washington, D.C.: United States Government Printing Office, 1966).

30. J.S. Coleman, T. Hoffer, and S. Kilgore. *Public and Private Schools: A Report to the National Center for Education Statistics by the National Opinion Research Center,* (Chicago: University of Chicago, 1981).

31. Ellis B. Page and Timothy Z. Keith. "Effects of U.S. Private Schools: A Technical Analysis of Two Recent Claims," *Educational Researcher,* vol. 10, no. 7 (August/September 1981), pp. 7–17.

32. Robert W. Heath and Mark A. Nielson, "The Research Basis for Performance-Based Teacher Education," *Review of Educational Research,* vol. 44, no. 4 (Fall 1974), p. 481.

33. Ronald G. Corwin, *A Sociology of Education* (New York: Appleton–Century–Crofts, 1965), p. 298.

34. Carolyn Denham and Ann Lieberman, eds. *Time to Learn* (Washington, D.C. National Institute of Education, 1980).

7. SCHOOL EFFORTS AND THE NEGATIVE SIDE OF NOBLE AMBITION

1. Dan C. Lortie, *Schoolteacher* (Chicago: The University of Chicago Press, 1975), p. 230.

2. Anneke E. Bredo and Eric R. Bredo, "A Case Study of Educational Innovation in a Junior High School: Interaction of Environment and Structure," *Research and Development Memorandum No. 132* (Stanford: Stanford Center for Research and Development in Teaching, 1975), pp. 16–17.

3. Roy R. Pellicano, New York City Public School Reform: A Line Teacher's View," *Phi Delta Kappan,* vol. 62, no. 3 (November 1980), p. 75.

4. J. Lloyd Trump and William Georgiades, "Which Elements of School Programs Are Easier to Change and Which Are Most Difficult—And Why?" *Bulletin of the National Association of Secondary School Principals,* vol. 55, no. 355 (May 1971), p. 56.

5. Roy A. Edelfelt, Ronald Corwin, and Elizabeth Hanna, *Lessons From the Teacher Corps* (Washington, D.C.: National Education Association, 1974), p. 59.

6. Michael W. Kirst, "Strengthening Federal-Local Relationships Supporting Educational Change" In Robert E. Herriott and Neal Gross, eds. *The Dynamics of Planned Educational Change* (Berkeley: McCutchan Publishing Corporation, 1979), p. 275.

7. Daniel L. Duke, Beverly Showers, and Michael Imber, *Teachers as School Decision Makers* (Project Report No. 80–A7, Institute for Research on Educational Finance and Governance, Stanford University, 1980).

8. Harry F. Wolcott, *Teachers Versus Technocrats* (Eugene, O. Center for Educational Policy and Management, University of Oregon, 1977), pp. 160–168.

9. Seymour Sarason, *The Culture of the School and the Problem of Change.*

10. Neal Gross, "Basic Issues in the Management of Educational Change Efforts." In Robert E. Herriott and Neal Gross, eds. *The Dynamics of Planned Educational Change* (Berkeley: McCutchan Publishing Corporation, 1978), p. 23.

11. William L. Smith, "Facing the Next Ten Years," *Journal of Teacher Education,* vol. 26, no. 2 (Summer 1975), p. 152.

12. Arthur L. Stinchcombe, "Social Structure and Organizations," in James G. March, ed. *Handbook of Organizations* (Chicago: Rand McNally, 1965), pp. 148–150.

13. Edelfelt, et. al., p. 47.

14. Sarason, *The Culture of the School . . . ,* p. 41.

15. A fascinating case study of this process can be found in Louis M. Smith and Pat M. Keith, *Anatomy of Educational Innovation* (New York: John Wiley & Sons, 1971). Also refer to the case studies of the Experimental Schools program contained in Robert

E. Herriott and Neal Gross, eds. *The Dynamics of Planned Educational Change* (Berkeley: McCutchan Publishing Corporation, 1979).

16. G. Thomas Fox, Jr., ed. "Federal Role in School Reform from Sociological and Educational Perspectives" (N.P., N.D.), p. 44.

17. Daniel Weiler, "A Public School Voucher Demonstration: The First Year of Alum Rock—Summary and Conclusions," In Gene V. Glass, ed. *Evaluation Studies Review Annual*, vol. 1 (Beverly Hills, CA: Sage Publication, 1976), p. 293.

18. Dan C. Lortie, *Schoolteacher* (Chicago: The University of Chicago Press, 1975), pp. 175–181.

19. Bredo and Bredo, p. 10.

20. Forrest Parkey, "Innovation in a Chicago Inner–City High School," *Phi Delta Kappan*, vol. 57, no. 6 (February 1976), p. 385.

21. Louis M. Smith and Pat M. Keith, *Anatomy of an Educational Innovation*, pp. 70–71 and 381–82.

22. In *Teachers Versus Technocrats* (Eugene Oregon: Center for Educational Policy and Management, University of Oregon, 1977), Harry F. Wolcott provides a case study of goal displacement. He describes how a well–intentioned effort to help educators demonstrate their accomplishments got "bogged down under the weight of a system that seemed to become an end in itself and a threat to those who bore the brunt of the effort" (p. 241).

23. Private communication with the late Professor Edward Begle, Stanford University School of Education.

24. "Weaknesses in Current Evaluation of Research," *Phi Delta Kappan*, vol. 51, no. 2 (October 1969), p. 103.

25. Egon G. Guba, "Problems in Utilizing the Results of Evaluation," *Journal of Research and Development in Education*, vol. 8, no. 3 (1975), p. 52.

26. Melvin Tumin, "Foreward," In Ronald G. Corwin, *Reform and Organizational Survival: The Teacher Corps as an Instrument of Educational Change* (New York: John Wiley, 1973), p. x.

27. Carolyn H. Denham, "Can Politicians Trust Evaluators? A Case Study of ECE Evaluation in California" *Phi Delta Kappan*, vol. 57, no. 8 (April 1976), p. 531.

28. Harry F. Wolcott, *Teachers Versus Technocrats*.

29. Ernest R. House. *The Politics of Educational Innovation* (Berkeley: McCutchan, 1974), p. 303.

8. TEACHERS HELPING TEACHERS—DOES THE PATIENT HAVE THE CURE?

1. Dan C. Lortie, *Schoolteacher*, pp. 75–76.

2. Ibid., pp. 192–196.

3. Ibid., p. 236.

4. Ibid., p. 195.

5. Ibid., pp. 142–143.

6. N.L. Gage, *Teacher Effectiveness and Teacher Education*, p. 173.

7. Susan Stavert Roper, Terrence E. Deal, and Sanford M. Dornbusch, *A Pilot Test of Collegial Evaluation for Teachers*, Research and Development Memorandum No. 142 (Stanford: Stanford Center for Research and Development in Teaching, 1976).

8. Thomas Toch, "Teachers Evaluate Teachers in Unusual Project in Toledo," *Education Week*, (October 27, 1982), p. 6.

9. Ibid.

10. Nancy Sigler Isaacson, *Secondary Teachers' Perceptions of Personal and Organizational Support During Induction to Teaching.* Ph.D. Dissertation, University of Oregon, August 1981, p. 137.

11. My appreciation to Dennis Lauro of the New York State United Teachers for information on the professional development concerns of teachers.

12. Cecil G. Miskel, et. al., "Organizational Structures and Processes, Perceived School Effectiveness, Loyalty, and Job Satisfaction," *Educational Administration Quarterly*, vol. 15, no. 3 (Fall 1979), pp. 97–118; Alice Z. Seeman and Melvin Seeman, "Staff Processes and Pupil Attitudes: A Study of Teacher Participation in Educational Change," *Human Relations*, vol. 29, no. 1 (1976), pp. 25–40.

13. Thomas Toch, "New Ideas, New Programs Fuel Reforms in Staff Development," *Education Week* (October 13, 1982), p. 7.

14. Duke, Showers, and Imber, 1980.

15. Ibid.

16. Dan C. Lortie, *Schoolteacher,* pp. 71–74.

17. Ibid., p. 72.

18. Susan Walton, "Study on Collective Bargaining Shows Moderate, Manageable Consequences," *Education Week*, vol. I, no. 33 (May 12, 1982), p. 1.

19. Ibid.

20. Ibid.

21. Teacher–Backed Candidates Won Big Last Fall; Schools to Benefit?" *Phi Delta Kappan*, vol. 57, no. 5 (January 1975), p. 375.

22. Seymour B. Sarason, "Again, the Preparation of Teachers . . . ," *Interchange*, p. 6.

23. Richard Wynn, "The Relationship of Collective Bargaining and Teacher Salaries, 1960 to 1980," *Phi Delta Kappan*, vol. 63, no. 4 (December 1981), p. 240.

24. Ibid.

25. Duke and Meckel, "The Slow Death of a Public High School."

26. Daniel L. Duke, Jon Cohen, and Roslyn Herman, "Running Faster to Stay in Place . . . "

27. Thomas Toch, "N.E.A. Supports Affirmative Action Over Seniority in Supreme Court Brief," *Education Week* (February 9, 1983), p. 7.

28. Eileen White, "Reagan, Four Education Officials Meet: N.E.A. Left Out of Talk on Teachers," *Education Week* (June 15, 1983), p. 1.

29. Myron Lieberman, "Teacher Bargaining: An Autopsy," *Phi Delta Kappan*, vol. 63, no. 4 (December 1981), pp. 231–234; Thomas A. Shannon, "Guidelines for Dismantling Collective Bargaining," *Phi Delta Kappan*, vol. 63, no. 4 (December 1981), p. 235.

30. Susan E. Staub, "Compulsory Unionism and the Demise of Education," *Phi Delta Kappan*, vol. 63, no. 4 (December 1981), pp. 235–236.

31. George H. Gallup, "The 14th Annual Gallup Poll of the Public's Attitudes Toward the Public Schools," *Phi Delta Kappan*, p. 44.

9. Rx for the Teaching Profession—Euthanasia or Rejuvenation?

1. Seymour Sarason, *Work, Aging, and Social Change.* Additional support for Sarason's thesis can be found in Chapter 1 of Donald A. Schön's *The Reflective Practitioner* (New York: Basic Books, Inc., Publishers, 1983).

2. The United States Army is concerned because it is rapidly shifting to field–based computers to guide military operations, but failing to attract recruits bright enough to use them effectively.

3. A description of this process as it took place in New York City appears in Daniel Duke, Jon Cohen, and Roslyn Herman, "Running Faster to Stay in Place . . . "

4. Daniel L. Duke and Adrienne M. Meckel, "The Slow Death of a Public High School."

5. George H. Gallup, "The 14th Annual Gallup Poll of the Public's Attitudes Toward the Public Schools," p. 39.

6. Gallup, p. 40; Alex Heard, "Poll Indicates Public Support for Education," *Education Week* (December 14, 1981), p. 6.

7. Eileen White, "Sputnik at 25," *Education Week* (October 13, 1982), p. 16.

8. Gallup, p. 41.

9. Sheppard Ranbom, "Educators Seek Solutions to 'Crisis' in Teaching," *Education Week* (March 2, 1983), p. 1.

10. Thomas Toch, "Houston Schools Pay Bonuses to Keep Teachers," *Education Week,* October 26, 1981, p. 1, 18.

11. Susan G. Foster, "Boston Seeks to Improve Teaching with Higher Standards, Cash Awards," *Education Week* (September 22, 1982), p. 6.

12. George W. Neill, "Higher Salaries Recommended for Teachers of Math, Science," *Education Week* (March 24, 1982), p. 8.

13. Victor S. Vance and Phillip C. Schlechty, "The Distribution of Academic Ability in the Teaching Force . . . ," p. 27.

14. Thomas Toch, "New Statistics Indicate Supply, Not Demand, May Cause Teacher Shortages in This Decade," *Education Week* (May 19, 1982), p. 14.

15. Arthur Blumberg and William Greenfield, *The Effective Principal* (Boston: Allyn and Bacon, Inc., 1980), p. 240.

16. Seymour Sarason, *Work, Aging, and Social Change,* p. 31.

17. Frederick J. McDonald, "Teaching in a Knowledge Society," *Alternative Futures in American Education,* Appendix 3 to Hearing on H.R.3606 and Related Bills to Create a National Institute of Education Before the Select Subcommittee on Education (Washington, D.C.: U.S. Government Printing Office, 1972), p. 269.

18. Victor G. Rosenblum, "High–Court Support for Professionalism in Education," *Education Week* (October 6, 1982), p. 24.

10. RECONCEPTUALIZING THE JOB OF TEACHING

1. Seymour Sarason, *The Culture of the School and the Problem of Change* (Boston: Allyn and Bacon, 1971).

2. In *The Effective Executive* (London: Pan Books, 1967), Peter Drucker discusses the problems that can result when organizations are staffed to avoid weaknesses rather than acquire strengths.

3. Robert L. Kahn, "The Work Module—A Tonic for Lunchpail Lassitude," *Psychology Today* (February 1973), pp. 35–36.

4. Ibid., p. 36.

5. Considerable research in the area of teaching and learning styles has been conducted by Professor Robert Spaulding of San Jose State University and Professor Bruce Joyce of San Francisco State University.

6. Bruce Joyce and Marcia Weil, *Models of Teaching* (Englewood Cliffs, N.J.: Prentice Hall, 1972).

7. Dan C. Lortie, *Schoolteacher,* p. 236.

8. For a rich description of one mastery program, refer to Robert Benjamin, *Making Schools Work* (New York: Continuum, 1981), pp. 39–68.

9. Jerome Bruner, "Schooling Children in a Nasty Climate," *Psychology Today,* vol. 16, no. 1 (January 1982), p. 59.

10. For a provocative look at coaches of pianists and Olympic swimmers, see Benjamin S. Bloom, "The Master Teachers," *Phi Delta Kappan*, vol. 63, no. 10 (June, 1982), pp. 664–668.

11. Nelson N. Foote, "The New Media and Our Total Society," *Alternative Futures in American Education*, appendix 3 to Hearings on H.R. 3606 and Related Bills to Create a National Institute of Education Before the Select Subcommittee on Education (Washington, D.C.: U.S. Government Printing Office, 1972), p. 223.

12. The author is indebted to Superintendent Alonzo Crim and, indirectly, to Mortimer Adler and his summer Great Books colloquia for ideas expressed in this section.

13. Thomas J. Sergiovanni, "The Context for Supervision." In Thomas J. Sergiovanni, ed. *Supervision of Teaching* (Alexandria, VA: Association for Supervision and Curriculum Development, 1982), p. 110.

14. Daniel L. Duke, "Leadership Functions and Instructional Effectiveness," *NASSP Bulletin*, vol. 66, no. 456 (October 1982), pp. 1–12.

15. Barry A. Farber and Julie Miller, "Teacher Burnout: A Psycho–educational Perspective" (Unpublished paper), p. 6.

16. Daniel L. Duke, *The Retransformation of the School* (Chicago: Nelson–Hall Publishers, 1978).

17. Dan C. Lortie, *Schoolteacher*, p. 242.

18. Brenda Biles, Lovely Billups, and Susan Veitch, "Bridging the Gap: The AFT Educational Research and Dissemination Program" (Paper presented at the Annual Meeting of the American Educational Research Association, April 1983).

19. "Effective–Schools Efforts Taking Root in the States," *Education Week* (September 22, 1982), p. 11.

20. Judith Warren Little, "Norms of Collegiality and Experimentation: Workplace Conditions of School Success," *American Educational Research Journal*, vol. 19, no. 3 (Fall 1982), pp. 325–340.

21. See, for example, the September 1982 issue of *Phi Delta Kappan*, vol. 64, no. 1, which is devoted to "Charting a New Course for Teacher Education."

22. Marlene Kramer, *Reality Shock: Why Nurses Leave Nursing* (St. Louis: C.V. Mosby Company, 1974).

23. Urie Bronfenbrenner, *Two Worlds of Childhood: U.S. and U.S.S.R.*

References

Alder, Christine; Bazemore, Gordon; and Polk, Kenneth. Delinquency in nonmetropolitan areas. In David Schichor and Delos H. Kelly (eds.), *Critical Issues in Juvenile Delinquency* (Lexington, Mass.: Lexington Books, 1980).

Anderson, Carolyn. The search for school climate: a review of the research. *Review of Educational Research*, vol. 52, no. 3 (Fall 1982), pp. 368–420.

Bardo, Pamela. The pain of teacher burnout: a case history. *Phi Delta Kappan*, vol. 61, no. 4 (December 1979), pp. 252–254.

Benjamin, Robert. *Making Schools Work* (New York: Continuum, 1981).

Biles, Brenda L.; Billups, Lovely H.; and Veitch, Susan C. Bridging the gap: the AFT Educational Research and Dissemination Program. Paper presented at the annual meeting of the American Educational Research Association, Montreal, 1983.

Bloch, Alfred M. Combat neurosis in inner-city schools. *American Journal of Psychiatry*, vol. 135, no. 10 (1978), pp. 1189–1192.

Bloch, Alfred M. and Bloch, Ruth Reinhardt. Teachers—a new endangered species? In Keith Baker and Robert J. Rubel (eds.), *Violence and Crime in the Schools* (Lexington, Mass.: Lexington Books, 1980).

Bloom, Benjamin S. The master teachers. *Phi Delta Kappan*, vol. 63, no. 10 (June 1982), pp. 664–668.

Blumberg, Arthur and Greenfield, William. *The Effective Principal* (Boston: Allyn and Bacon, Inc., 1980).

Bredo, Anneke E. and Bredo, Eric R. A case study of educational innovation in a junior high school: interaction of environment and structure. Research and development memorandum no. 132 (Stanford: Stanford Center for Research and Development in Teaching, 1975).

Bronfenbrenner, Urie. *Two Worlds of Childhood: U.S. and U.S.S.R.* (New York: Pocket Books, 1973).

Broudy, Harry S. *The Real World of the Public Schools* (New York: Harcourt Brace Jovanovich, Inc., 1972).

Brown, B. Frank. A study of the school needs of children from one-parent families. *Phi Delta Kappan*, vol. 61, no. 8 (April 1980), pp. 537–540.

Bruner, Jerome. Schooling children in a nasty climate. *Psychology Today*, vol. 16, no. 1 (January 1982), pp. 57–63.

Bruno, James E. and Doscher, Lynn. Analysis of teacher transfers in a large urban school district. Paper presented at the annual meeting of the American Educational Research Association, San Francisco, 1979.

Campbell, Roald F. The professorship in educational administration—a personal view. *Educational Administration Quarterly*, vol. 17, no. 1 (Winter 1981), pp. 1–24.

Centre, John A. and Potter, David A. School and teacher effects: an interrelational model. *Review of Educational Research*, vol. 50, no. 2 (Summer 1980), pp. 273–291.

Cerra, Frances. Stress buffeting older teachers now in schools. *New York Times* (October 14, 1980), p. 81.

Charters, W.W., Jr. Some factors affecting teacher survival in school districts. In Donald Gerwin (ed.), *The Employment of Teachers* (Berkeley: McCutchan Publishing Corporation, 1974).

Cohen, David K. and Neufeld, Barbara. High school education and the progress in education. Paper presented at the Daedalus/St. Paul's Conference on Secondary Education, February 1981.

Coleman, James S., et. al. *Equality of Educational Opportunity* (Washington, D.C.: United States Government Printing Office, 1966).

Coleman, James S.; Hoffer, T.; and Kilgore, S. *Public and Private Schools: A Report to the National Center for Education Statistics by the National Opinion Research Center* (Chicago: University of Chicago Press, 1981).

Conant, James Bryant. *The Education of American Teachers* (New York: McGraw-Hill Book Company, 1963).

Corwin, Ronald G. *A Sociology of Education* (New York: Appleton-Century-Crofts, 1965).

Crowe, Patrick H. *How to Teach School and Make a Living at the Same Time* (Kansas City: Sheed Andrews and McMeel, Inc., 1978).

Cuban, Larry. Persistent instruction: the high school classroom, 1900–1980. *Phi Delta Kappan*, vol. 64, no. 2 (October 1982), pp. 113–118.

Cuban, Larry. Teacher and community. *Harvard Educational Review*, vol. 39, no. 2 (Spring 1969), pp. 253–272.

Dearman, Nancy B. and Plisko, Valena White. *The Condition of Education, 1980 Edition* (Washington, D.C.: National Center for Educational Statistics, U.S. Government Printing Office, 1980).

Denham, Carolyn H. Can politicians trust evaluators? a case study of ECE evaluation in California. *Phi Delta Kappan*, vol. 57, no. 8 (April 1976), pp. 530–531.

Denham, Carolyn H. and Lieberman, Ann (eds). *Time to Learn* (Washington, D.C.: National Institute of Education, 1980).

Dillon-Peterson, Betty (ed.). *Staff Development/Organization Development* (Alexandria, Va.: Association for Supervision and Curriculum Development, 1981).

Doyle, Walter. Are students behaving worse than they used to behave? *Journal of Research and Development in Education*, vol. 11, no. 4 (Summer 1978), pp. 3–16.

Drucker, Peter. *The Effective Executive* (London: Pan Books, Ltd., 1970).

Duke, Daniel L. Environmental influences on classroom management. In Daniel L. Duke (ed.), *Classroom Management*, The Seventy-eighth Yearbook of the National Society for the Study of Education (Chicago: University of Chicago Press, 1979).

Duke, Daniel L. *The Retransformation of the School* (Chicago: Nelson-Hall Publishers, 1978).

Duke, Daniel L.; Cohen, Jon; and Herman, Roslyn. Running faster to stay in place: New York City schools face retrenchment. *Phi Delta Kappan*, vol. 63, no. 1 (September 1981), pp. 13–17.

Duke, Daniel L. and Jones, Vernon F. Two decades of discipline—assessing recent efforts to reduce student behavior problems. Paper presented at the annual meeting of the American Educational Research Association, Montreal, 1983).

Duke, Daniel L. and Meckel, Adrienne M. The slow death of a public high school. *Phi Delta Kappan*, vol. 61, no. 10 (June 1980), pp. 674–677.

Duke, Daniel L. and Meckel, Adrienne M. *Teacher's Guide to Classroom Management* (New York: Random House, 1984).

Duke, Daniel L.; Showers, Beverly K.; and Imber, Michael. Teachers and shared decision making: the costs and benefits of involvement. *Educational Administration Quarterly*, vol. 16, no. 1 (Winter 1980), pp. 93–106.

Duke, Daniel L.; Showers, Beverly K.; and Imber, Michael. Teachers as school decision makers. Project Report No. 80-A7 (Stanford: Institute for Research on Educational Finance and Governance, 1980).

Dunathan, Arni T. Teacher shortage: big problems for small schools. *Phi Delta Kappan*, vol. 62, no. 3 (November 1980), pp. 205–206.

Dworkin, Anthony Gary. The changing demography of public school teachers: some implications for faculty turnover in urban areas. *Sociology of Education*, vol. 53, no. 2 (April 1980), pp. 65–73.

Eckland, Bruce K. College entrance examination trends. In Gilbert R. Austin and Herbert Garber (eds.), *The Rise and Fall of National Test Scores* (New York: Academic Press, 1982).

Edelfelt, Roy A.; Corwin, Ronald; and Hanna, Elizabeth. *Lessons from the Teacher Corps* (Washington, D.C.: National Education Association, 1974).

Educational Research Service. *Measuring Trends in Salaries and Wages in Public Schools: ERS Composite Indicator of Changes* (Arlington, Va.: Educational Research Service, Inc., 1979).

Elam, Stanley M. and Gough, Pauline B. Comparing lay and professional opinion on Gallup Poll questions. *Phi Delta Kappan*, vol. 62, no. 1 (September 1980), pp. 47–48.

Elkind, David. *The Hurried Child: Growing Up Too Fast Too Soon* (Reading, Mass.: Addison-Wesley Publishing Company, 1981).

Farber, Barry A. and Miller, Julie. Teacher burnout: a psychoeducational perspective. Unpublished paper.

Flach, Frederic. *Choices* (Philadelphia: J. B. Lippincott Company, 1977).

Foote, Nelson N. The new media and our total society. In *Alternative Futures in American Education*. Appendix 3 to Hearings on H.R. 3606 and Related Bills to Create a National Institute of Education Before the

Select Subcommittee on Education (Washington, D.C.: U.S. Government Printing Office, 1972).

Fox, G. Thomas (ed.). Federal role in school reform from sociological and educational perspectives. Unpublished paper.

Freeman, John and Hannan, Michael T. Growth and decline processes in organizations. *American Sociological Review,* vol. 40 (Apri 1975), pp. 215–228.

Gage, N. L. *Teacher Effectiveness and Teacher Education* (Palo Alto, Ca.: Pacific Books, Publishers, 1972).

Gallup, George H. The 12th Annual Gallup Poll of the Public's Attitudes Toward the Public Schools. *Phi Delta Kappan,* vol. 62, no. 1 (September 1980), pp. 33–46.

Gallup, George H. The 14th Annual Gallup Poll of the Public's Attitudes Toward the Public Schools. *Phi Delta Kappan,* vol. 64, no. 1 (September 1982), pp. 37–50.

Getzels, J. W. Paradigm and practice: on the impact of basic research in education. In Patrick Suppes (ed.), *Impact of Research on Education: Some Case Studies* (Washington, D.C.: National Academy of Sciences, 1978).

Godwin, J. *Murder USA: The Ways We Kill Each Other* (New York: Ballantine Books, 1978).

Grant, W. Vance and Lind, C. George. *Digest of Education Statistics 1979* (Washington, D.C.: National Center for Education Statistics, U.S. Government Printing Office, 1979).

Gross, Neal. Basic issues in the management of educational change efforts. In Robert E. Herriott and Neal Gross (eds.), *The Dynamics of Planned Educational Change* (Berkeley: McCutchan Publishing Corporation, 1979).

Guba, Egon G. Problems in utilizing the results of evaluation. *Journal of Research and Development in Education,* vol. 8, no. 3 (1975), pp. 40–58.

Guthrie, James W. and Zusman, Ami. Teacher supply and demand in mathematics and science. *Phi Delta Kappan,* vol. 64, no. 1 (September 1982), pp. 28–33.

Heath, Robert W. and Nielson, Mark A. The research basis for performance-based teacher education. *Review of Educational Research,* vol. 44, no. 4 (Fall 1974), pp. 463–484.

Hedin, Diane and Conrad, Dan. Changes in children and youth over two decades: the perceptions of teachers. *Phi Delta Kappan,* vol. 61, no. 10 (June 1980), pp. 702–703.

Herriott, Robert E. and Gross, Neal. The complex nature of educational change. In Robert E. Herriott and Neal Gross (eds.), *The Dynamics of Planned Educational Change* (Berkeley: McCutchan Publishing Corporation, 1979).

House, Ernest R. *The Politics of Educational Innovation* (Berkeley: McCutchan Publishing Corporation, 1974).

Isaacson, Nancy Sigler. *Secondary Teachers' Perceptions of Personal and Organizational Support during Induction to Teaching.* Ph.D. dissertation, University of Oregon, August 1981.

Johnson, Susan Moore. Performance-based staff layoffs in the public schools: implementation and outcomes. *Harvard Educational Review*, vol. 50, no. 2 (May 1980), pp. 214–233.

Joyce, Bruce and Weil, Marcia. *Models of Teaching* (Englewood Cliffs, N.J.: Prentice-Hall, 1972).

Joyce, Bruce; Brown, Clark C.; and Peck, Lucy. *Flexibility in Teaching* (New York: Longman, 1981).

Kahn, E. J. *The American People* (Baltimore: Penguin Books Inc., 1975).

Kahn, Robert L. The work module—a tonic for lunchpail lassitude. *Psychology Today* (February 1973), pp. 35–39, 94–95.

Keniston, Kenneth. Do Americans really like children? *Today's Education*, vol. 64, no. 4 (Nov-Dec 1975), pp. 16–21.

Kirst, Michael W. Strengthening federal-local relationships supporting educational change. In Robert E. Herriott and Neal Gross (eds.), *The Dynamics of Planned Educational Change* (Berkeley: McCutchan Publishing Corporation, 1979).

Koerner, James D. *The Miseducation of American Teachers* (Baltimore: Penguin Books, 1965).

Kramer, Marlene. *Reality Shock: Why Nurses Leave Nursing* (St. Louis: C. V. Mosby Company, 1974).

Lasch, Christopher. *The Culture of Narcissism* (New York: W. W. Norton & Company, Inc., 1978).

Levin, Henry. A cost-effectiveness analysis of teacher selection. In Donald Gerwin (ed.), *The Employment of Teachers* (Berkeley: McCutchan Publishing Corporation, 1974).

Lieberman, Myron. Teacher bargaining: an autopsy. *Phi Delta Kappan*, vol. 63, no. 4 (December 1981), pp. 231–234.

Lisman, David. Should continuing education be mandated? *American Educator*, vol. 4, no. 2 (Summer 1980), pp. 29–31.

Little, Judith Warren. Norms of collegiality and experimentation: workplace conditions of school success. *American Educational Research Journal*, vol. 19, no. 3 (Fall 1982), pp. 325–340.

Lortie, Dan C. *Schoolteacher* (Chicago: The University of Chicago Press, 1975).

McDonald, Frederick J. Teaching in the knowledge society. In *Alternative Futures in American Education*. Appendix 3 to Hearings of H.R. 3606 and Related Bills to Create a National Institute of Education Before the Select Subcommittee on Education (Washington, D.C.: U.S. Government Printing Office, 1972).

McGuire, William H. Teacher burnout. *Today's Education*, vol. 68, no. 4 (1979), pp. 5–7.

McLaughlin, Milbrey Wallin and Marsh, David D. Staff development and school change. *Teachers College Record*, vol. 80, no. 1 (September 1978), pp. 69–94.

Mednick, Sarnoff A. Primary prevention of juvenile delinquency. In David Schichor and Delos H. Kelly (eds.), *Critical Issues in Juvenile Delinquency* (Lexington, Mass.: Lexington Books, 1980).

Miskel, Cecil G.; Fevurly, Robert; and Stewart, John. Organizational structures and processes, perceived school effectiveness, loyalty, and job satisfaction. *Educational Administration Quarterly*, vol. 15, no. 3 (Fall 1979), pp. 97–118.

Murnane, Richard J. Interpreting the evidence on school effectiveness. Unpublished manuscript, 1980.

Murray, John M. Narcissism and the ego ideal. *Journal of the American Psychoanalytic Association*, vol. 12 (1964), pp. 477–511.

National Education Association. *Status of the American Public School Teacher, 1975–76* (Washington, D.C.: NEA Research, 1977).

National Institute of Education. *Violent Schools—Safe Schools*, The Safe School Study Report to the Congress, Volume I (Washington, D.C.: National Institute of Education, 1978).

Newell, R. C. Teacher stress. *American Teacher* (Dec 1978/Jan 1979), pp. 16–17.

Newman, Joan and Graeme. Crime and punishment in the schooling process: a historical analysis. In Keith Baker and Robert J. Rubel (eds.), *Violence and Crime in the Schools* (Lexington, Mass.: Lexington Books, 1980).

Norman, Jan and Harris, Myron. *The Private Life of the American Teenager* (New York: Rawson, Wade Publishers, Inc., 1981).

Page, Ellis B. and Keith, Timothy Z. Effects of U.S. private schools: a technical analysis of two recent claims. *Educational Researcher*, vol. 10, no. 7 (Aug/Sept 1981), pp. 7–17.

Parkay, Forrest. Innovation in a Chicago inner-city high school. *Phi Delta Kappan*, vol. 57, no. 6 (February 1976), pp. 384–390.

Pellicano, Roy R. New York City public school reform: a line teacher's view. *Phi Delta Kappan*, vol. 62, no. 3 (November 1980), pp. 174–177.

Perry, Cheryl L. *Adolescent Behavior and Criminogenic Conditions in the Culture of the High School.* Ph.D. dissertation, Stanford University, 1980.

Reed, John Shelton. *Available Evidence on Public Attitudes toward Education* (Princeton, N.J.: Advisory Panel on the Scholastic Aptitude Test Score Decline, College Entrance Examination Board, 1977).

Report on Conflict & Violence in California's High Schools (Sacramento: California State Department of Education, 1973).

Roper, Susan Stavert; Deal, Terrence E.; and Dornbusch, Sanford M. *A Pilot Test of Collegial Evaluation for Teachers*, Research and Development Memorandum No. 142 (Stanford: Stanford Center for Research and Development in Teaching, 1976).

Ruchkin, Judith P. Does school crime need the attention of policemen or educators? *Teachers College Record*, vol. 79, no. 2 (1977), pp. 225–244.

Rutter, Michael; Maughan, Barbara; Mortimore, Peter; and Ouston, Janet. *Fifteen Thousand Hours* (Cambridge, Mass.: Harvard University Press, 1979).

Sarason, Seymour B. Again, the preparation of teachers: competency and job satisfaction. *Interchange*, vol. 10, no. 1 (1978/79), pp. 1–11.

Sarason, Seymour B. *The Culture of the School and the Problem of Change* (Boston: Allyn and Bacon, Inc., 1971).

Sarason, Seymour B. *Work, Aging, and Social Change* (New York: The Free Press, 1977).

Schlechty, Phillip C. and Vance, Victor S. Do academically able teachers leave education? the North Carolina case. *Phi Delta Kappan*, vol. 63, no. 2 (October 1981), pp. 106–112.

Schlechty, Phillip C. and Vance, Victor S. Recruitment, selection and retention: the shape of the teaching force. Paper presented at Conference on Research on Teaching, Airlee House, February 1982.

Schon, Donald A. *The Reflective Practitioner* (New York: Basic Books, Inc., Publishers, 1983).

Seabrook, Jeremy. *What Went Wrong?* (New York: Pantheon Books, 1978).

Seeman, Alice Z. and Melvin. Staff processes and pupil attitudes: a study of teacher participation in educational change. *Human Relations*, vol. 29, no. 1 (1976), pp. 25–40.

Sergiovanni, Thomas J. The context of supervision. In Thomas J. Sergiovanni (ed.), *Supervision of Teaching* (Alexandria, Va.: Association for Supervision and Curriculum Development, 1982).

Shannon, Thomas A. Guidelines for dismantling collective bargaining. *Phi Delta Kappan*, vol. 63, no. 4 (December 1981), p. 235.

Smith, B. Othanel. Pedagogical education: how about reform? *Phi Delta Kappan*, vol. 62, no. 2 (October 1980), pp. 87–91.

Smith, David C. and Street, Sue. The professional component in selected professions. *Phi Delta Kappan*, vol. 62, no. 2 (October 1980), pp. 103–107.

Smith, Louis M. and Keith, Pat M. *Anatomy of an Educational Innovation* (New York: John Wiley, 1971).

Smith, William L. Facing the next ten years. *Journal of Teacher Education*, vol. 26, no. 2 (Summer 1975), pp. 150–152.

Staub, Susan E. Compulsory unionism and the demise of education. *Phi Delta Kappan*, vol. 63, no. 4 (December 1981), pp. 235–236.

Stephens, J. M. *The Process of Schooling* (New York: Holt, Rinehart and Winston, Inc., 1967).

Stinchcombe, Arthur L. Social structure and organizations. In James G. March (ed.), *Handbook of Organizations* (Chicago: Rand McNally, 1965).

Supranovich, Beth Bond. Differentiated staffing revisited. *Phi Delta Kappan*, vol. 64, no. 1 (September 1982), pp. 20–21.

Survey of Violence in Schools Occurring from 1964 through 1968 (Washington, D.C.: U.S. Government Printing Office, 1970).

Thomas, W.I. and E.S. *The Child in America* (New York: Knopf, 1928).

Trump, J. Lloyd and Georgiades, William. Which elements of school programs are easier to change and which are most difficult—and why? *Bulletin of the National Association of Secondary School Principals*, vol. 55, no. 355 (May 1971), pp. 54–68.

Tumin, Melvin. Foreword. In Ronald G. Corwin, *Reform and Organizational Survival* (New York: John Wiley, 1973).

Tyack, David B. *Turning Points in American Educational History* (Lexington, Mass.: Xerox College Publishing, 1967).

Tyack, David B. and Berkowitz, Michael. The man nobody liked: toward a social history of the truant officer, 1840–1940. *American Quarterly,* vol. 29, no. 1 (Spring 1977), pp. 31–54.

U.S. Bureau of the Census. *Historical Statistics of the United States, Part 1* (Washington, D.C.: U.S. Bureau of the Census, U.S. Government Printing Office, 1975).

Vance, Victor S. and Schlechty, Phillip C. The distribution of academic ability in the teaching force: policy implications. *Phi Delta Kappan,* vol. 64, no. 1 (September 1982), pp. 22–27.

Wallin, H.A. The educational employment histories of the professional workforce in B.C. schools, 1968–69 (Vancouver: Center for the Study of Administration in Education, the University of British Columbia, 1971).

Wangberg, Elaine G.; Metzger, Devon J.; and Leviton, Justin E. Working conditions and career options lead to female elementary teacher job dissatisfaction. *Journal of Teacher Education,* vol. 33, no. 5 (Sept/Oct 1982), pp. 37–40.

Weaver, W. Timothy. In search of quality: the need for talent in teaching. *Phi Delta Kappan,* vol. 61, no. 1 (September 1979), pp. 29–32, 46.

Weaver, W. Timothy. Projecting teacher needs and professional staffing patterns for the mid-1980's. Paper presented at the annual meeting of the American Educational Research Association, Boston, 1980.

Weiler, Daniel. A public school voucher demonstration: the first year of Alum Rock—summary and conclusions. In Gene V. Glass (ed.), *Evaluation Studies Review Annual,* Volume 1 (Beverly Hills, Ca.: Sage Publications, 1976).

Whitener, Joy E. *An Actuarial Approach to Teacher Turnover.* Ph.D. dissertation, Washington University, 1965.

Wise, Arthur E. Why educational policies often fail: the hyperrationalization hypothesis. *British Journal of Curriculum Studies,* vol. 9, no. 1 (1977), pp. 43–57.

Wolcott, Harry F. *Teachers Versus Technocrats* (Eugene, Or.: Center for Educational Policy and Management, University of Oregon, 1977).

Wynn, Richard. The relationship of collective bargaining and teacher salaries, 1960 to 1980. *Phi Delta Kappan,* vol. 63, no. 4 (December 1981), pp. 237–242.

Yarger, S.J.; Howey, K.R.; and Joyce, B.R. *Inservice Teacher Education* (In press).

Index